# Effective Services for Young Children

## Report of a Workshop

Lisbeth B. Schorr, Deborah Both,
and Carol Copple, Editors

National Forum on the Future of Children and Families
National Research Council
Institute of Medicine

National Academy Press
Washington, D.C. 1991

Library of Congress Catalog Card No. 91-62826
International Standard Book Number 0-309-04579-7

Additional copies of this report are available from:
National Academy Press
2101 Constitution Avenue N.W.
Washington, D.C. 20418

S-440
Printed in the United States of America

# Preface

The Workshop on Effective Services for Young Children, held November 1 and 2, 1990, was one in a series of events that the National Forum on the Future of Children and Families has sponsored on current and emerging child and family policy issues. A joint project of the National Research Council's Commission on Behavioral and Social Sciences and Education and the Institute of Medicine, the forum was established in 1987 to promote an ongoing dialogue among scholars and experts in children and family issues and leaders in government, business, philanthropy, and the media. The forum provides a neutral setting for discussion of problems affecting children and families and the development of policy options and strategies to improve their health and well-being. Its mission is to enhance the policy-making capacity of the public and private sectors on behalf of children and families.

The forum's Working Group on Effective Services organized the workshop in response to evidence of a growing consensus that:

• The nation has an enormous stake in reversing the alarming deterioration of the circumstances in which poor and otherwise disadvantaged children grow up.

• Many past efforts to reverse unfavorable trends in damaging outcomes such as school failure, adolescent childbearing, substance abuse, and violent crime have been relatively ineffective.

• Much new knowledge on how to improve the institutions and programs that are meant to strengthen children and families is now available but is not being used.

• Most of the difficult unsolved problems call for remedies that cut across multiple systems and disciplines.

The forum is well situated to bring together the range of individuals and interests needed to sort through and extract from current knowledge and activities the options and strategies that could achieve major improvements in services for young children and their families. Accordingly, the forum convened a two-day workshop involving 60 invited participants to assess the state of current knowledge and to identify strategies for action. Participants included many of the nation's leaders in current efforts to improve services for children and families and many who are at the forefront of attempts to understand these efforts in the context of current experience, theory, and research. A list of participants is included in the appendix.

The presentations and discussions that took place during the two-day meeting, together with the background papers, enriched participants' understanding of available options and steps that could be taken to improve the well-being of the nation's children and their families through more effective services. Needless to say, however, not all important aspects of the provision of effective services for children were covered in this initial workshop.

With this summary of our workshop deliberations, we hope to reach a wider audience of policy makers, administrators, and practitioners. We hope that this summary and the background papers will inform future efforts to ensure that all American children and their families will benefit from the high-quality education, social services, health care, and family support services that are within the nation's capacity to provide.

The forum is grateful for the contributions of the impressive array of workshop participants and to the authors of the background papers. We are also grateful to the Carnegie Corporation of New York, which provides general support to the forum, andto the Foundation for Child Development, which has provided funding for the publication and dissemination of this report. We extend our thanks to Carol Copple, a valued consultant and one of the drafters of the summary. In addition, we wish to express appreciation to Deborah Both, the forum's senior research associate, and Drusilla Barnes, administrative secretary, for their dedicated efforts in organizing the meeting and for producing this report.

> Lisbeth B. Schorr, *Chair*
> Forum Working Group
>   on Effective Services
>   for Young Children
>
> Julius B. Richmond, *Chair*
> National Forum on the Future
>   of Children and Families

# Contents

# Effective Services for Young Children

# Report of the Workshop

# Effective Services for Young Children

The Workshop on Effective Services for Young Children was based on the premise that a great deal is now known about how to make early education, health programs, and social services more effective, especially for the populations most dependent on good public services, who have not been well served in the past. A second assumption was that local communities are having a hard time improving services within the context of existing institutional and bureaucratic structures. The hope was that a group of thoughtful and well-informed individuals, representing both the public and private sectors, could identify strategies to improve the effectiveness of programs and policies for young children and families.

The workshop began with a review of the attributes of programs that had improved outcomes for disadvantaged children and discussion of the implications for making systems more hospitable to effective programs. Lessons from past attempts to accomplish similar goals were then considered. Following this discussion, participants considered promising strategies to modify how services are organized and financed, how practitioners and program managers are trained, how programs are held accountable, and how services are coordinated. The need for expanded public understanding of the nature of both problems and solutions was emphasized.

One question participants struggled with throughout the workshop was the extent to which various groups of the population could be expected to benefit from similar strategies. Participants seemed to concur that different interventions were needed for different populations. Three overlapping populations were identified: (1) all children who live in poverty at some time during their childhood (comprising about 30 percent of all children); (2) all children who come to the attention of public agencies as requiring special help (7-10 percent of all children); and (3) all those who live in geographic areas of concentrated poverty and social dislocation (comprising about 10 percent of poor children). Although there certainly is overlap, the strategies that would improve outcomes among the three groups are not identical.

All poor children could benefit from more accessible and higher-quality health care, expanded and improved child care, and more effective schools and social services. Improved income support programs, including expanded earned income tax credits, and job training and placement should also benefit these children and their families. Most participants recognized a need for economic policies and other measures to increase incomes of poor families in addition to services, and they opposed the idea of supporting one approach (i.e., benefits versus services) over the other.

Most participants agreed that the most pressing problems seemed to be among children with multiple needs, including children in families who are unlikely to be lifted out of poverty and disadvantage solely by income supports or improvements in the general economy. Services for these children, and for the children and families who fall into the population of what has been called the truly disadvantaged, were the primary focus of most of the workshop discussion.

A second recurrent contextual theme concerned the weaknesses of current services. There was broad agreement that most services tend to be fragmented, categorical, inaccessible, episodic, arbitrary, and unresponsive to family needs. Services are generally late, too narrow, too shallow, and too impersonal and give too little attention to families, neighborhoods, and communities. Observations and anecdotes were offered to confirm the ineffectiveness of services for children and families.

## ATTRIBUTES OF EFFECTIVE SERVICES

The past 25 years have yielded substantial information about what makes services for children and families successful. The background paper by Lisbeth Schorr draws on the book, *Within Our Reach: Breaking the Cycle of Disadvantage* (Schorr, 1988), which described and analyzed the operation of some 17 programs in the fields of family planning, prenatal care, child health, child welfare/family support, child care and preschool education, and elementary school education, all of which had shown evidence of reducing rates of damaging outcomes or their antecedent risk factors among disadvantaged children.

The nature of the evidence Schorr employed for determining what programs were effective combined relevant quantitative data with other kinds of information from theory, research, and experience. This meta-analytic approach, which includes but is not confined to quantitative data, makes it possible to make rigorous and informed judgments about what has worked in the past and what is likely to work in the future, even among complex, multifaceted and interactive interventions.

The workshop discussion suggested considerable agreement that the following attributes, identified in the paper, account for the effectiveness of successful programs.

• *Successful programs are comprehensive, flexible, and responsive.* They take responsibility for providing easy and coherent access to services that are sufficiently extensive and intensive to meet the major needs of those they work with. They overcome fragmentation through staff versatility, flexibility, and active collaboration across bureaucratic and professional boundaries.

• *Successful programs deal with the child as an individual and as part of a family, and with the family as part of a neighborhood and a community.* Most successful programs have deep roots in the community and respond to needs perceived and identified by the community. They tend to work with two, and often three, generations, collaborating with parents and local communities to create programs and institutions that respond to unique needs of different individuals and populations.

• *Staff in successful programs have the time, training, skills, and institutional support necessary to create an accepting environment and to build relationships of trust and respect with children and families.* They work in settings that allow them to develop meaningful one-to-one relationships, and to provide services respectfully, ungrudgingly, and collaboratively. Moreover, front-line workers in these programs are given the same respect, nurturing, and support by program managers that they are expected to extend to those they serve.

• *Programs that are successful with the most disadvantaged populations persevere in their efforts to reach the hardest-to-reach and tailor their services to respond to the distinctive needs of those at greatest risk.* Many of the programs providing health, education, and social services to multiply disadvantaged children and families find it essential to combine these services with the supports traditionally provided by families.

• *Successful programs are well managed, usually by highly competent, energetic, committed and responsible individuals with clearly identifiable skills and attitudes.* Contrary to the common belief that great charisma is essential for running a successful program, managers of effective programs have identifiable attributes that can be learned and systematically encouraged, such as a willingness to experiment and take risks, to tolerate ambiguity, and to allow staff to make flexible, individualized decisions.

• *Successful programs have common theoretical foundations that undergird their client-centered and preventive orientation.* Staff of these programs believe in what they are doing. Effective programs seek to replace the prevailing preoccupation with failure and episodic intervention with an orientation that is long-term, preventive, and empowering.

Some observers have concluded that programs that incorporate these attributes will never become available to large numbers of low-income families because such programs typically exist outside or at the margins of large human service systems and are therefore difficult to replicate. The Schorr paper suggested an alternate conclusion: that if these attributes are what it takes for success, systematic exploration is required of how prevailing policies and practices could be changed to support and encourage the adoption of these attributes in all programs and systems serving poor and otherwise disadvantaged children and families.

Before examining the strategies that could create the needed systems change, the workshop participants considered what might be learned from earlier large-scale reform efforts.

## LESSONS OF THE PAST AND STRATEGIES
## FOR THE FUTURE

Efforts of the last three decades to restructure human service systems and the lessons that emerge were presented by Peter Edelman and Beryl Radin. In their paper on this topic, they described the Community Action Programs (CAP) of the Office of Economic Opportunity and the Model Cities Program of the Department of Housing and Urban Development, which were developed in the 1960s to create mechanisms to deliver services to the underserved more effectively than existing institutions. Some of the CAP agencies, including Head Start, thrived and survived; other parallel, federally funded, "untethered" agencies did not survive but succeeded temporarily as yardsticks against which the performance of existing programs could be measured and as goals to push old-line agencies to do better. The CAP legacy also included a group of people "who were nurtured, learned to use the system, and went on to community leadership."

The Model Cities Program was designed to pull together existing categorical programs at the local level to make them more responsive to the needs of the poor. The model cities concept of combining education, health, and social services with housing and physical renewal was crushed almost before the program was launched as a result of dissipated authority and radically reduced funds. When the inadequate resources were spread over 66 cities rather than the 4 to 6 originally intended, the potential for making a difference was destroyed.

Nonetheless, the efforts of the 1960s, when divested of the caricatures and rhetoric with which they have been surrounded, carry some clear lessons for the 1990s:

• Government at all levels has a role, but cannot do its job without the participation of other institutions, agencies, and individuals. The federal government exercises its greatest influence by how it *pays for* services. Local and perhaps state governments have important roles in the *coordination* of services. One important but neglected government role is "to help rediscover and rebuild the sense of community that we have lost in too many places."

• Major problems cannot be solved without money, but money won't do the job unless deeper structural failings are confronted. "Measures to make services comprehensive, accessible, and better coordinated . . . will miss their mark unless they are accompanied by adequate funding, . . . better education and training, . . . and changes in personnel policies . . . ." Basic institutions that make up a community must be restored. New program designs require "a balancing of professional and community involvement that eluded reformers in the 1960s."

• There are interventions that work, but they must be coordinated and combined, even though it is difficult to get the political decision-making system to act in comprehensive terms, since decision-making responsibility is fragmented. Furthermore, there are few multiservice interest groups, and fragmentation and inaccessibility serve the function of rationing utilization. Mechanisms that overcome fragmentation include multiservice centers, service centers attached to schools, reinvented settlement houses, and offices or bureaus that coordinate services for children and youth.

• Place-specific models could play a fundamental role in rebuilding a feeling of neighborhood and community, especially in areas of intense poverty. "A fully funded, highly targeted, comprehensive approach in an area of great poverty has never really been tried." A coordinated effort, according to Edelman and Radin, should not only include comprehensive and responsive services and schools, but should also attend to housing, public safety, and economic development, allowing these interventions to build on one another to achieve a visible level of effectiveness. They conclude by calling for "a few demonstrations that are comprehensive on a synergistic scale never before attempted."

This last proposal elicited considerable discussion. Participants emphasized that if such demonstrations were undertaken, it would be important from the beginning to set up financing arrangements as parts of existing systems, so that successful demonstrations could be readily expanded to additional communities. The chances of success could also be enhanced by establishing a center that would provide the respected auspices and the insulation from outside pressure to put coherence and discipline into related sets of demonstration programs, e.g., an entity such as the Manpower Demonstration and Research Corporation, which bridges politics, policy making, and the social sciences.

Whether such projects should be funded through a political jurisdiction, such as a county or city, or through a local institution (e.g., a school, a community development corporation, a community health center, or a public/private intermediary organization) was the subject of debate. In any case, it was emphasized that the public bureaucracies, as well as the private sector, must be included from the outset.

It was also suggested that the difficulties such a complex, multifaceted program would encounter in maintaining a clear sense of mission would have to be taken into account. Participants acknowledged that such a saturation strategy would be a formidable task, with a significant risk of failing in at least some of the sites. The chance of success would be increased if the target communities had an existing base of strong local institutions, networks, and leadership, along with a degree of commitment from the business community.

Political realities were also brought into the discussion. The fact that areas of concentrated poverty are not spread evenly throughout the states creates a political obstacle for any strategy that focuses on problems affecting only a few states. It was pointed out that seven states have 50 percent of this country's children, and the most serious problems of children and families are even more concentrated; for instance, one out of three foster children lives in New York or California. This does not mean that geographically targeted strategies should not be attempted; it simply means that garnering the necessary political support, especially at the federal level, will not be easy.

## STRATEGIES TO ENCOURAGE SYSTEMS CHANGE

Considerable agreement emerged around the contention that successful programs could not be made available to all who need them without substantial change occurring in large systems and institutions. The challenge is to make these institutions and systems hospitable to and supportive of the essential attributes of effective programs. Most participants also seemed to believe that in most circumstances the time for launching additional small-scale, program-specific demonstrations may be past, and that among the most critical tasks ahead was to take successful programs to scale.

Consideration of how this might be done occupied most of the workshop participants' energies. Several strategies aimed at institutional and systems change to improve programs for disadvantaged children and their families were discussed, including changes in financing, training and technical assistance, coordination and collaboration, the use of outcome measures, and efforts to create greater public understanding. Although each of these strategies was considered at separate sessions, participants in each session made it clear that these strategies had to be combined so their impact would be interactive, for none would be effective in isolation.

For example, the discussion of financing strategies made clear that the best innovations in financing methods could not make up for insufficient funds. However, additional funds are unlikely to be obtained without better evidence that programs achieve socially desired outcomes and without more effective public education. Participants in the session on training agreed that traditional professional training may contribute to but does not cause fragmented, discontinuous, and ineffective services. Both improved financing arrangements and a shift to outcome accountability could do much to support new skills and new attitudes on the part of practitioners. The session on collaboration emphasized the contribution that flexible funding, staffing, and cross-disciplinary training could make to successful collaboration and coordination.

In this summary and in the seven background papers, the various strategies are considered individually; the reader should keep their interdependence in mind.

## New Financing Strategies

The background papers on financing, written by Frank Farrow and Drew Altman, emphasized that methods of financing services directly affect the nature and outcomes of services by shaping priorities and incentives and by influencing how useful services are to families. More flexible and more permanent funding arrangements could do much to make services more effective and to reinforce new and improved policy directions. However, both authors agreed that without sufficient levels of funding, no financing methods can ensure adequate services.

The Farrow paper points out that most effective programs incorporate multiple funding sources and cut across traditionally separate service domains. The paper describes funding innovations of several kinds that are beginning to occur at the state level. The most basic approach involves joint funding of services across agency lines in order to achieve common goals. Agencies share the costs of services that they would otherwise provide independently, thus reinforcing a common policy direction and increasing the likelihood of more coordinated service delivery at the local level. Cross-agency financing of this type is a modest step, but it has real benefits at the local level and represents a step toward more flexible, less categorical financing.

States have also evolved new ways of using federal entitlement programs to expand the funding base available for children and families. They use federal entitlements, such as Medicaid dollars, to cover as broad a range of services as federal law will allow and as state budgets can accommodate. As an example of how entitlement sources could be tapped in new ways, the Altman paper proposed that states designate school-based services programs as participating Medicaid providers, since the large majority of young people using school-based health and human services programs are Medicaid-eligible. These funds could make a significant contribution to stabilizing school-based projects and reaching more of the underserved.

States are also claiming federal entitlements more aggressively for costs previously paid entirely by state and local funds, thus freeing those state and local funds for reinvestments in service system improvements. For instance, by expanding Title IV-E claims to the maximum extent allowed under federal law, states can dramatically increase available funds.

Yet another strategy being used by a growing number of states is frontline service financing through use of flexible dollars. In this approach, funds are allocated to meet families' individual needs at the actual point of delivery; practitioners have discretion in the use of a specified sum of money to purchase goods or services to help accomplish a family's goals.

A fourth strategy aims at greater flexibility in the use of state-appropriated funds to meet family needs, with authority over those funds delegated to local entities. This strategy is a more fundamental shift from centralized, usually categorical state decision making toward more flexible local control over funding decisions. Iowa's broad decategorization initiative in two demonstration counties is an example of this strategy.

In considering strategies to overcome the perceived ill effects of categorical funding—such as that it tends to undercut efforts to provide comprehensive, coordinated services, workshop participants identified certain risks and limitations attached to the decategorization of funding streams. As the Altman paper points out, decategorization can do little to add dollars to an underfunded system and may not save as much money as is often claimed. Moreover, categorical programs have traditionally been better able to rally the political support necessary to obtain greater funding and to resist the budget ax. Despite these concerns, many participants viewed decategorization as a useful step in improving services for families and children and proposed several specific actions to encourage decategorization.

The Altman paper also suggested federal action to promote integrated funding streams and services integration through a little-known entity called the Low-Income Opportunity Advisory Board (LIOAB). The LIOAB, established by President Reagan, brings together in the White House all the federal agencies responsible for the major social programs. According to Altman, "the LIOAB has the authority not just to tinker with categorical programs, but to help effect the thoroughgoing changes necessary to enable states and communities to pool financing, to reorganize services, and, generally, to change the rules and try out new approaches."

Using the LIOAB, the President could launch a national integrated services initiative, establishing guidelines, soliciting proposals from states and communities, and providing necessary waivers and pooled funding. If the White House chose not to take that role, the Department of Health and Human Services could take the lead.

Other proposals to encourage decategorization were also considered, including provision for the evaluation of demonstration efforts and the funds to support them.

## New Emphasis on Practice-Based Training for Practitioners and Managers

The paper by Douglas Nelson on the role of training and technical assistance suggests that, if provider-client interactions are to become more collaborative and family-centered, with greater flexibility and discretion, practitioners and managers must acquire new perspectives and new skills. New forms of preservice education and in-service training are needed, which emphasize: (1) the family context in assessing and addressing problems and providing support; (2) the communication and interaction skills that encourage trust and mutuality between provider and client; and (3) the diagnostic skill and knowledge about resources that enable practitioners to take broader responsibility for identifying and addressing the diverse range of problems that families experience.

These areas must be addressed more effectively in the curricula of professional schools as well as in practice-based training; they must also be central to the ongoing supervision and evaluation that serve as an important form of continuing training to workers on the job.

Training practitioners to be comfortable and skilled in situational, collaborative, interactions is a different enterprise than teaching people how to follow certain set procedures. The skills needed to deal with clients effectively situation-by-situation are difficult to reduce to textbooks or practice manuals; rather, they are more effectively taught through case illustrations, observation of actual practice by experienced workers, and constructive criticism of work in actual service settings.

The Nelson paper proposes that, in the provision of such training, exemplary service settings and programs clearly have a key role to play as learning centers. Although participants differed on the particulars of this role, no one questioned the importance of practice-based training. The use of exemplary programs as training sites was appealing for three major reasons. First, practice-based and experiential learning is pedagogically sound, especially for learning the kinds of skills and attitudes in question. Second, programs identified as learning centers because of their exemplary practice would get the kind of visibility and recognition that would encourage them and expand their influence. Third, initially it is probably easier to change the content and orientation of training programs in practice sites than in academic institutions.

A serious practical issue for practice-based training is whether there would be enough field opportunities in exemplary programs to provide the training that is seen as desirable. At the present time, according to participants, not even the minimal quantity and quality of practice-based training sites are available. Training large numbers of front-line service providers in exemplary programs requires public- and private-sector investment to greatly expand practice-based training.

Participants urged that colleges and universities be encouraged to undertake much more cross-disciplinary training. Some participants were quite skeptical about the possibility of making changes in academic institutions of the breadth and depth that are needed. Others were more optimistic, arguing that even academic institutions are market-driven. It was acknowledged, however, that such change will take time and will require a gradual shift in perceptions of acceptable training by students, practitioners, and the institutions in which they work.

Perhaps the greatest risk is "pseudo-change" within the academic institutions and other organizations who do training. Because of categorical funding, turf issues, and inertia, institutions might simply co-opt the new perspective and claim to be teaching new skills without actually making major changes in the content of their curricula.

### Expanded Technical Assistance Capacity

Participants agreed that a greatly expanded technical assistance capacity is needed, both nationally and regionally, to provide state and local administrators and managers with the requisite level of fiscal, organizational, and political expertise to change organizational cultures and institutional environments.

Today most administrators of human service programs lack familiarity with the interplay and intricacies of the funding streams that shape the amount and kind of services available. They are seldom prepared to develop or adopt a shift toward the use of outcome measures in accountability systems and evaluation. And most policy makers and administrators have too little training and skill in the arts of public and political education that are critical to changing services for children and families.

These crucial skills, abilities, and interest could be brought more fully into the efforts to improve services by increasing the cadre of national consultants who can provide technical assistance in support of state and local efforts. A start has been made in such initiatives as the Clark Foundation's Technical Assistance Forum, but a far larger and broader technical capacity is critically needed.

The long-run objective is to build at state and community levels a greater level of knowledge and experience in affecting the larger environments in which services are delivered. One relatively untapped resource to help reshape the capacity of institutional and policy environments is individuals with administrative and policy-level positions who have many of the requisite abilities, but lack the conventional credentials. For example, hospitals and nursing homes recruit retiring Medicaid directors for their experience and skill in manipulating state organization and fiscal environments. Given the urgent need, it was judged important not to overlook those who already have the ability and experience to make significant change in institutional and policy environments.

One proposal that generated considerable interest among participants was to encourage the creation of regional centers or other intermediaries to provide technical assistance to state and local governments and to groups of providers. These centers or intermediaries would offer assistance related to the changing of the organizational culture and provide expertise in financing, management information systems, collaborative strategies, leadership development, and the use of outcomes-based approaches. Intermediaries like the Ounce of Prevention in Illinois and Florida, and Friends of the Family in Maryland, seem to be successful in nurturing local programs, buffering them from bureaucratic and political pressures, interpreting the needs of the programs to state officials, providing training and technical assistance, and furnishing program managers and policy makers with information that can lead to more responsive programs and policies.

Participants emphasized the need to be specific and detailed in the objectives of technical assistance, as well as in the training of workers. Otherwise, the frequent vagueness of training goals for workers ("Let's get someone to talk about counseling") will also pervade technical assistance efforts ("Let's get someone to talk about financing"). This level of detail, it was emphasized, is far from sufficient for equipping individuals to move large systems and institutions through extensive and dramatic changes.

From the discussion emerged a sense that the capacity and the incentives to develop new thinking about the provision of effective services are missing. New mechanisms and institutions are needed to promote more systematic, more strategic, and less random approaches to encouraging, supporting, evaluating, and learning from current and future efforts to improve services for disadvantaged children and families.

## Active Collaboration and Coordination
## Across Professional Bureaucratic Boundaries

At the workshop, the working definition of collaboration was simply "people of different organizations working together." Collaboration is not an end in itself, participants stressed; it is only worthwhile as a means to an end. A major reason for collaboration is that no single system can effectively help the children and families in greatest need of services, because they are likely to have multiple and interrelated problems that spill over traditional bureaucratic boundaries.

Despite increasing recognition of the need for collaboration and coordination, these attributes are not widely achieved or, for that matter, attempted. The obstacles to collaboration are numerous and complex. Rigid bureaucracies, past practices, and categorical funding streams head the list of barriers. In addition, teachers, social workers, medical personnel, mental health clinicians, and other professionals and service providers have different educational backgrounds, speak different languages, and look to their own professions for recognition, respect, and promotion.

Furthermore, when several programs with different missions begin to collaborate, outside observers may fear that each of the participating programs is neglecting its core mission. In addition, many of the present mechanisms for accountability operate against collaboration. Services to children and families in the United States exist in multiple governmental jurisdictions, and thus multiple lines of accountability. Accountability is defined narrowly in most cases, since measuring the goals of narrow missions is far easier than measuring the goals of integrated missions.

Finally, organizational change is particularly hard for large organizations and systems when they are operating in tight fiscal environments and having great difficulty performing their respective missions. Most people in service systems today do not even have the time and resources to perform their core functions, much less to invest in the process of change and a broad consideration of their mission. At present, the major systems serving children and families are, as one participant put it, "persistently failing organizations."

Nonetheless, across the nation there are examples of organizations that have surmounted these obstacles. Based on an analysis of successful collaborations, the following characteristics appear to be important (for greater detail see the paper by Olivia Golden):

• *Redefined and overlapping missions.* Collaborating organizations have succeeded in developing overlapping conceptions of mission and in enlarging agency missions beyond conventional limits.

• *Conflict resolution.* In effective collaborations, people recognize that conflict between the organizations will not disappear and develop ongoing mechanisms for resolving conflict.

• *Commitment of administration time.* Managers and administrators in successful collaborations devote considerable time and attention to collaboration, spending time looking out from their organizations rather than simply up or down within them.

• *Importance of personal relationships.* Collaboration seems to thrive when managers and front-line staff cultivate personal relationships as a basis for collaboration.

• *Exchange relationships.* Collaborating agencies have some basis for exchange, something they can do for each other.

• *Involvement of those served and a broad spectrum of the community.* Such involvement at all stages of the collaboration appears to be key to success.

Participants noted that in promoting collaboration, there is an underlying tension between restructuring systems or focusing on creating viable linkages and joint projects between systems as they exist currently. In the successful collaborations to date, there is activity on both levels. Participants suggested it is probably not necessary to choose one route or the other.

Several participants observed that collaboration and coordination among health and social services, welfare departments, and schools are unlikely to progress far in the absence of financial and other incentives from all levels of government.

Participants voiced support for actions encouraging states and cities to experiment with partnerships in which the city takes responsibility for services to children and the state agrees to support that responsibility. To begin, a mayor might convene and get involved in a community-wide process of assessing needs. The New Beginnings effort in San Diego is an example of such an approach.

One participant suggested the creation of a cabinet-level position (e.g., Secretary of Children's Services) and similar positions at the state, county, and city government levels. Funds and programs dealing with children (particularly poor children from birth to six), now housed in various other government agencies, would be redirected into this department. Alternatively, a variety of federal funding streams would pass through a Children's Services Office, where they would be blended into services and programs that deal with children and their families in a more holistic way.

Participants' views differed on what it meant to make reforms from the top down or from the bottom up, but there seemed to be agreement that efforts that go in both directions simultaneously are most effective.

## Greater Emphasis on Using Outcome Measures to Ensure Accountability

Within public education and human services, the primary question asked of practitioners is: "Did you do what you were told to do?" This question is reflected in the nature of performance evaluation, in the forms that personnel at all levels are asked to fill out, and in the defense offered to account for failure: ("I taught them, but they didn't learn!")

The paper by David Hornbeck on outcome measures argues that results must control practice. The right question is "Did it work?" Trying hard and following a set of prescribed procedures are no longer enough. In the view of workshop participants, outcomes measurement is an important tool of systems change and improved performance of providers. It may also become a precondition for obtaining additional funds and more flexible funding arrangements.

Signs of growing outcomes orientation are emerging in public education and, to a lesser extent, in other sectors. The national education goals and objectives for the year 2000, established by the President and the governors, reflect this orientation. The National Education Goals Panel will issue an annual report card on the states, and Congress is considering a bill to establish a similar report card panel. An outcomes-based strategy is central to the Business Roundtable's 10-year commitment to join each of the states in changing the process and product of education. An aggressive outcome strategy has been legislated in Kentucky and is being considered in other states. Outcomes approaches are emerging outside education, as in the Public Health Service's Year 2000 health objectives for the nation.

Certain features essential to an outcomes based approach are outlined in the Hornbeck paper. First, it is important to examine the underlying assumptions that "provide the lens through which one will identify the outcomes to be achieved." For instance, in education, a critical assumption is that all children can learn at significantly higher levels.

Next, it is essential to identify the outcomes that the program or system is expected to produce with children and families. The expectation level of outcomes defines the results: if little is expected, little will be accomplished; if expected outcomes are high, much can be achieved. For each outcome area, measurable indicators must be defined.

Third, assessment strategies must be as rich as the outcomes one wishes to achieve. Outcomes that are not measured will soon become irrelevant. For instance, the educational outcome of students' acquiring strong writing skills probably will not be achieved if assessment is done only through multiple choice testing.

The fourth essential feature of an outcomes-based approach, and the most controversial, is attaching consequences to success or failure in achieving results. Incentives for success and disincentives for failure must be a routine part of the system. And those held accountable, particularly those closest to the clients, pupils, patients, or families, must have the power to decide what strategies are used to accomplish the objectives.

It is not sufficient simply to define high-expectation outcomes and attach consequences to success or failure in achieving them. Those who are accountable for achieving the outcomes must have the capacity to do so, which means substantial changes in preservice and in-service training. A number of other enabling conditions also will be necessary for success. For instance, Kentucky considers the following conditions necessary for desired educational outcomes: prekindergarten for all disadvantaged children, a family resource center in every elementary school with 20 percent or more poor children, and a youth service center in every secondary school with 20 percent or more poor students.

Although community-wide commitment to defining and achieving outcomes for children and families was seen as important, workshop participants stressed that particular institutions—not just the community in general—must be held accountable for results. The operation of these institutions and the results they achieve will be powerfully changed by an outcomes-based approach.

## Complementary Functions of Outcomes Assessment and Evaluation

Participants distinguished between outcomes assessment, which documents results (i.e., we got from Point A to Point B), and evaluation, which tells us how the program results were achieved. Evaluation also illuminates what elements of an intervention actually made a difference. For instance, outcome assessment for a prenatal care program, which might include rates of infant mortality, low birthweight, and other measures of infant and maternal well-being, would be intended to answer the basic question of whether the prenatal care worked. An evaluation design would attempt to determine the effectiveness of certain specific components of the program, such as childbirth classes or smoking cessation intervention. However, it was noted that it is important to keep in mind that many interventions seem to be effective because their multiple components work interactively. In these instances, a detailed, "thick" description may be the best guide to how the intervention produced desired outcomes.

Well-designed evaluations can make use of the new interest in face-valid outcome measures and provide contextual information that helps in interpreting outcome data. For instance, outcome measures may indicate that, after a two-year initiative to reduce adolescent pregnancy, the teenage pregnancy rate had risen. Evaluation data may reveal that the percentage of low-income families in the area rose over the two-year period, that pregnancies increased at a greater rate among comparison groups not targeted by the program, or other factors that help to explain the rising rates.

Clearly, an outcomes approach carries political risks as well as benefits. On the positive side, centering political debates around outcomes can be a good way of mobilizing support. But political support may be eroded when outcomes are less favorable than expected, even when exogenous factors are the cause. The shift toward wider and more appropriate use of outcome measures would be helped along, one participant suggested, by an "honest politician's guide to outcome measures and evaluation." Such a guide would include warnings that an unthinking application of outcome measures, such as undue reliance on standardized tests or a misunderstanding of the impact of such exogenous factors as the changing population of a community, could have unfortunate results.

Some participants warned of the danger of relying on outcomes assessment unless the shift to emphasizing outcomes is also embedded in an overall approach that shapes all key components. According to Hornbeck, these components include:  substantial control by those held accountable; appropriately rich assessment measures; staff development; and the enabling conditions needed to realize the specified outcomes. With this caveat, participants were enthusiastic about the potential of an outcomes approach improving systems toward more effective services.

### New and Expanded Efforts to Educate
### the Public and Policy Makers

A panel of participants (James Comer, Richard Wehling, Kati Haycock, and Ann Rosewater) presented remarks on the need for better public understanding of these important, complex issues and how it might be brought about.

Survey data from the Advertising Council's campaign on Breaking the Cycle of Disadvantage indicate that a large proportion of the public does not have a fundamental understanding about the current conditions or urgent needs of America's children and families, particularly those who are poor. Even when there is awareness of the issues and concern, people often feel immobilized by the magnitude of the problem and by the belief that outcomes are fully under individual control, with no need for a supportive environment.

Public education efforts will be more effective, the panelists suggested, if these efforts articulate a vision of what might be, describe obstacles to achieving the vision, include evidence of strategies and programs that work, and document that the costs of inaction exceed the costs of appropriate action. More people need to understand that changes in the economy require a higher level of education and social skills today than in previous generations and, furthermore, that systematic social action, including governmental action, can make a difference. These messages must be accompanied by the recognition that there are no quick, cheap fixes or solutions. Patience and the adoption of a long-term perspective are essential components of any public education effort, since the real impact of effective services must be viewed intergenerationally.

## CONCLUSION

Today there is a ferment of activity and experimentation in states and local communities to improve the circumstances of children and families, especially the disadvantaged. Reform is under way in each of the systems serving children and families—health, education, social services, and family support. Consensus is emerging, as this workshop illustrated, on many of the directions in which the nation could move to provide more effective services to children and families.

Workshop participants identified some options and strategies for creating the changes needed to make services effective—not just here and there, for children and families served by a few exemplary programs, but for large numbers of families served by mainstream service systems. Innovative ideas in the areas of training and technical assistance, financing, collaboration, outcomes measurement, and public education were debated individually and in the context of systems change.

A clear theme was the need for multiple interactive approaches to improving services for children and families. Participants considered it unwise to prescribe a single approach to improving services for young children. The overwhelming sentiment seemed to be that changing circumstances should guide choices between major systemic reforms and incremental change within existing systems; between improving and expanding programs operating within the mainstream of public systems and those operating under "protective bubbles"; and between measures to benefit the majority of poor children and families and the subset of the population whose future is most dependent on improved services. Similarly, participants were wary of prescribing a single local institution as the one around which more effective services should be organized.

At the same time, participants agreed on the major attributes of effective programs and favored more concerted efforts to bring about needed changes in major institutions and systems. They also concluded that the workshop deliberations should become part of continuing systematic endeavors to encourage the kind of changes in policies and practices that could result in vastly improved outcomes for the nation's children.

# Background Papers

# Attributes of Effective Services for Young Children: A Brief Survey of Current Knowledge and Its Implications for Program and Policy Development

*Lisbeth B. Schorr*
School of Medicine, Harvard University
with
*Deborah Both*
National Research Council

The purpose of this paper is to set the stage for consideration of strategies to improve services for young children by the workshop participants. It focuses on what is known about the attributes of services that seem to be effective in changing outcomes for children who have been least well served in the past, in the belief that effective policies and strategies must accurately reflect what is known about what works at the level of the local program, where the service or support meets the client/participant/pupil/patient/family.

The first section describes briefly where the services, programs, and interventions under consideration fit within antipoverty policy and the broader range of social policies for children and families. The second section addresses the question of how one can make reasonable judgments about whether programs are successful and about the program attributes that seem to be essential. The third section describes a set of attributes that seem to characterize effective programs. The final section is an attempt to tease out some of the implications of current findings about the attributes of effective programs, perhaps the most important of which is that the development, spread, and successful operation of effective programs requires changes in the systems within which programs are funded, held accountable, evaluated, and within which they recruit and retain personnel.

## THE POLICY CONTEXT

The services, programs, and interventions that are the focus of this paper are a subset of the broader range of antipoverty policies and other social policies needed to improve outcomes for children and families in the United

*23*

States today. Among the concerns that have prompted increasing public anxiety, and that seem to have stimulated interest in communities throughout the country to take action to improve the conditions of children and families, are the following:

• High rates of childhood poverty.
• High rates of single-parent families, school-age childbearing, and welfare dependency.
• High rates of school dropout and school failure.
• Lack of skilled, motivated workers to keep the U.S. economy productive and competitive.
• High rates of drug and alcohol abuse and family disintegration; children growing up abused, neglected, unsupervised, and ill prepared to benefit from schooling.
• High rates of violence; high social costs of rising rates of imprisonment and violent crime.
• An increasingly polarized society, a growing gap between the haves and have-nots, the existence of populations that may remain permanently and intergenerationally outside the mainstream of U.S. society.

All of these problems are interrelated. Effective responses to any of these problems can be expected to ameliorate each of them. However, effective remedies are not entirely interchangeable. Most notably, income poverty, the category of disadvantage which affects the largest number of children and families in the United States,[1] will respond to economic solutions, whereas other forms of disadvantage will not respond to economic solutions alone.[2]

Somewhere between one-fifth and one-third of poor children, who have

---

[1]See Bane and Ellwood (1989); National Center for Children in Poverty (1990); Danziger and Stern (1990).

[2]Studies of youth employment have found that "improvements in the national economy will not solve the chronic and concentrated unemployment among a subgroup of the youth population. . . . Whatever happens to the economy overall, a significant number of youth (especially poor and minority youth) cannot find or remain in jobs and are likely to experience chronic joblessness as adults" (Hahn and Lerman, 1985).

In its section on "The Truly Disadvantaged," the W.T. Grant Foundation Commission on Work, Family, and Citizenship (1988) concluded that those most likely to suffer from persistent poverty and an "ominous future" were single mothers and chronically nonemployed young men. The commission recommended that identifying and removing the antecedent risk factors was society's "most cost efficient chance of reducing the stacked odds" for these young people and recommended toward this end "comprehensive, flexible, and coordinated services beginning early in life including family planning, prenatal health care, preparent training, continuing parent counseling and support, nutritional services, child care, early childhood education, and health education."

been called the truly disadvantaged, are unlikely to be lifted out of poverty by a rising economic tide or to be helped significantly by income policies alone (such as an expanded Earned Income Tax Credit, a higher minimum wage, or stronger child support programs). These children must be helped to escape poverty through a range of interventions, some of which would raise the current incomes of the families in which they live, and some of which would raise in other ways their chances of school success, of productive, well-paid employment, and of being able to create stable families of their own.

Although the families in which these children live are found in both urban and rural areas, they are becoming increasingly concentrated in inner-city neighborhoods characterized by high rates of single-parent families, school dropout, early unmarried childbearing, long-term welfare dependency, unemployment, violent crime, social isolation, and inadequate schools and services (Wilson, 1987).

Improved health, education, and social services would raise the chances of a productive life for all children, particularly for all poor children. For the most disadvantaged children, improved services are essential to buffer them from the most serious consequences of their accumulated risks. Even expanded economic opportunities may remain beyond the reach of young people whose health has been neglected, whose early lives have left them without hope, and whose education has failed to equip them with essential skills.

In neighborhoods where persistent poverty and social dislocation are concentrated, the absence of good services and schooling have actually become additional risk factors for this generation as well as the next. The institutions and services now in place have not interrupted the downward spiral for these children or ameliorated the consequences of their poverty, because needed services are typically inaccessible, of poor quality, or simply do not exist. Available services are often the wrong ones, too cumbersome to reach, too fragmented, too late, too meager, or too narrow in scope. With a few noteworthy exceptions, the children who, along with their families, need the attention of the most skilled, experienced, and wise professionals, the best organized and best funded institutions and agencies, and the most comprehensive services, are dependent on doctors, clinics, social agencies, child care, and schools that are tragically overwhelmed, and offer the worst and the least.

The absence of good services has contributed to the perpetuation of the intergenerational effects of disadvantage. The educational and service interventions that could raise the odds that youngsters will succeed at school and be equipped with the skills they need to become productively employed at jobs that could support a family—which would in turn increase their chances of avoiding too early parenthood and of being able to form stable families (Danziger and Stern, 1990; Furstenberg et al., 1987; McLanahan, 1988; Plotnick, 1987)—are typically missing.

We now have it within our power to interrupt this cycle. A persuasive body of research and experience shows that the knowledge exists on which to build the interventions that will significantly improve outcomes among children and youth at risk, including the children who are truly disadvantaged.

## THE BURDEN OF PROOF: WHAT IS THE NATURE OF THE EVIDENCE THAT WE SHOULD CONSIDER PERSUASIVE?

More than 20 years ago, when social policy was formulated in an atmosphere of boundless optimism, the combination of a little theoretical research, fragments of experience, and a lot of faith and dedication were enough to justify a new social program. Today budget deficits, fears of wasting money and perpetuating dependency, ambivalence about helping the poor, and a gloomy sense of social problems beyond solution have combined to reinforce demands for tangible evidence of effectiveness as a condition for support of any social program.

Several obstacles complicate the search for such evidence. The attempt to achieve the quantitative precision of research in the biological and physical sciences has interfered with meaningful evaluation of many kinds of human services. The pursuit of quantitative elegance has been particularly destructive in the evaluation of programs for the disadvantaged, because the very elements that make these programs effective among disadvantaged populations pose the greatest hurdles to the evaluator.

Programs offering a broad array of individualized interventions, which may be most powerful in their interaction and which have multiple outcome objectives, may be anathema to the evaluator faced with the task of designing a manageable and precise evaluation plan. Often the scope of the inquiry becomes unduly narrow—many evaluation efforts attempt to identify a single effective ingredient in an immensely complex and interactive system. They tend to measure what can readily be measured and may miss the effect of the intervention on more crucial outcomes. For example, the first evaluation of Head Start measured only IQ changes, despite the fact that the purposes of the program included increasing social competence, parent involvement, and improved access to health, nutrition, and social services.

In the interests of achieving clear evaluation results, the ability of successful programs to respond to the particular needs and desires of a given community or client population is often diminished by pressures to implement interventions that are uniform across sites or to incorporate centrally designed program elements.

Other important elements of successful programs (such as that services are provided respectfully and ungrudgingly, in an atmosphere that is supportive and caring) are hard to standardize, measure, and document or even to describe in words that mean the same thing to different persons.

Because of the difficulty in measuring significant outcomes, many evaluation efforts limit themselves to measuring or describing *processes* (Do participants attend, do they express satisfaction with the program, do providers express satisfaction with the program?) These process indicators, or interim outcome measures, can be extremely useful in both policy development and program management—especially when research has provided relevant information that reliably links process indicators and outcome measures. Without such information, however, process measures are unlikely to be persuasive to skeptical policy makers.

The combination of these obstacles is formidable, but they need not be paralyzing. In making judgments about what works, the human services field could use some of the insights coming out of the management literature, which suggest that American business has often been handicapped by its practices of considering as facts only the data one can put numbers on; assuming that a truly rational analysis bypasses "all the messy human stuff"; and achieving precision by so reducing the scope of what is analyzed that the most important questions are ignored (Peters and Waterman, 1982).

Approaches that combine relevant quantitative data with other kinds of information from theory, research, and experience across domains should make it possible to make rigorous and informed judgments about what has worked in the past and what is likely to work in the future, even among complex, multifaceted, and interactive interventions.

There is little argument that the pressures of politics and the needs for immediate action on urgent social problems force policy and program people to draw conclusions from less rigorous information than they, or the researchers they rely on, might wish for. The disagreement comes around the question of how rigorous the methodology must be, about how precise a quantification of both inputs and outcomes is required, to assure those relying on the findings that they are not being misled.

The approach taken in this paper combines information from theory, research, and experience from such different domains as preschool, primary, and secondary education; health care; child care; social services; family support; and job training. It combines informed judgments with a synthesis of quantitative data to the extent they are available and seems to reflect program operations and outcomes sensibly and accurately. One can think of this as a meta-analytic approach that includes but is not confined to quantitative data. Table 1 displays some of the available quantitative data on effectiveness from the domains of family planning, prenatal care, preschool education, and family support.

By moving beyond isolated assessments of program effectiveness and

**TABLE 1** Quantitative Effects of Selected Interventions

| Intervention | Sponsor | Outcome |
|---|---|---|
| **School-based health clinic** St. Paul, Minnesota. 1973-present. | St. Paul-Ramsey Co. Medical Center | Childbearing among female students in first two participating high schools decreased by more than 50% within three years. (Edwards et al., 1977, 1980) |
| **School-related health clinic** serving junior and senior high school with all black, low-income student bodies, totaling over 1,700 students. Baltimore, Maryland. 1982-1984. | Johns Hopkins University School of Medicine | Among 695 female respondents (of whom about 3/4 were sexually active), the proportion of sexually active 9th-12th grade girls who became pregnant declined by 25%; rate in comparison school went up 58% in same period. (Zabin et al., 1986) |
| **Comprehensive prenatal care** for 744 school-age pregnant girls, mostly black and single, all poor. Baltimore, Maryland. 1979-1981. | Johns Hopkins University School of Medicine | Low birth weight (<2,500 gm) rate among participants:  9.9%* among comparison group: 16.4% Very low birth weight (<1,500 gm) rate among participants:  1.9% among comparison group: 3.9% (Hardy, 1981) |
| **Comprehensive prenatal care** for 7,000 low-income women in 13 California counties. 1979-1982. | California State Department of Health | Low birth weight (<2,500 gm) rate among participants:  4.7%* among comparison group: 7.0% Very low birth weight (<1,500 gm) rate among participants:  0.5% among comparison group: 1.3% (Korenbrot, 1984) |
| **Homevisiting** to 305 pregnant teenagers by lay "Resource Mothers" in rural South Carolina. 1981-1983. | South Carolina State Health Department | Low birth weight (<2,500 gm) rate among participants:  10.0%* among comparison group: 13.0% Very low birth weight (<1,500 gm) rate among participants:  1.0% among comparison group: 4.5% (Unger and Wandersman, 1985) |

**TABLE 1** *Continued*

| Intervention | Sponsor | Outcome |
|---|---|---|
| **Nurse visiting of high-risk mothers** during pregnancy and for 2 years after birth (Participants and controls selected by random assignment). Elmira, New York. 1978-1983.<br><br>(Comparisons are with randomly assigned controls.) | University of Rochester Medical School | Among poor, unmarried women:<br>Returned or completed school, 10 months after giving birth:<br>participants: 75%<br>controls: 50%<br>Subsequent pregnancies 4 years after first birth:<br>One-half as many among participants as among controls.<br>Abuse or neglect among children:<br>participants: 4%<br>controls: 19%<br>Among 14 - 16 year olds: participants had babies weighing an average of one pound more than controls.<br>Among mothers who smoked:<br>Premature births: 2%<br>participants: 10%<br>controls:<br>(Olds et al., 1986) |
| **Comprehensive health, child care and social services** for 18 infants aged 0-2 1/2 and their families. New Haven, Connecticut. 1968-1972. | Yale University Child Study Center | At 10-year follow up:<br>Average years of education completed by mother:<br>participants: 13.0<br>comparison: 11.7<br>Average number of children in family:<br>participants: 1.67<br>comparison: 2.2<br>Proportion of families self-supporting:<br>participants: 86%<br>comparison: 53%<br>Children with serious school problems:<br>participants: 28%<br>comparison: 69%<br>(Seitz et al., 1985) |

**TABLE 1** *Continued*

| Intervention | Sponsor | Outcome |
| --- | --- | --- |
| **Intensive in-home crisis and family-preservation services.** Tacoma and Seattle, Washington. 1974 to present (evaluation, 1983-1985) | Catholic Children's Services and Homebuilders | In 88% of families in which removal of child was imminent when intervention began, family was intact and child had not been removed one year later. (Kinney et al., 1977; E.M. Clark Foundation, 1985) |
| **Preschool education and weekly home visits** over two-year period for 3- and 4-year-old randomly assigned poor black children. Ypsilanti, Michigan. 1962-present (evaluation of 1962-1964 participants). | The Perry Preschool Program High/Scope | Of 121 responding at age 19: Partic. Control; Employed 59% 32%; H.S. Grad 67% 49%; Post H.S. Ed. 38% 21%; Arrested 31% 51%; Of 112 responding: Years in spec. ed. 16% 28%; Among 49 females: T.A. Preg. 32% 59% (Berrueta-Clement et al., 1984) |
| **Summer preschool education and weekly home visits during remainder of year,** for black 3-5-year olds and their mothers. Murfreesboro, Tennessee. 1962-1965. | The Early Training Project Peabody Teachers College | At age 21, one-third more dropouts in comparison group than among participants; control children placed in special education classes at six times the rate of participating children. (Gray, et al., 1983; Lazar et al., 1982) |
| **Changing elementary school climate** through applying principles of child development and basic management; new relationships among principal, teachers, parents. New Haven, Connecticut. 1968-present. | Yale University Child Study Center | At outset, intervention schools ranked 32nd and 33rd of 33 New Haven elementary schools in reading, math, attendance, and behavior. 15 years later, with no change in SES of students, demonstration schools ranked 3rd and 5th in test scores, had no serious behavior problems. One had best attendance record in city 4 of previous 5 years. (Comer, 1985, 1988) |

**TABLE 1** *Continued*

| Intervention | Sponsor | Outcome |
|---|---|---|
| **Intensive intervention with 1,000 low birth-weight infants** in 8 cities, including comprehensive pediatric care, weekly (first year) or biweekly (thereafter) home visits, parent meetings, and care in a special child development center. 1985-1988. | Robert Wood Johnson Foundation | At age 3, participants had IQ scores that averaged 13.2 points higher (heavier babies) and 6.6 points higher (smaller babies) than randomly matched controls; their mothers reported significantly few behavior problems than did mothers of the controls. (Infant Health and Development Program, 1990) |
| **Early intervention programs using home visitors** with available outcome data in Texas, South Carolina, and Illinois were visited and reviewed by GAO. Review completed in 1990. | General Accounting Office | Results included improvement in mental and physical development, health, parent-child interaction, and home environment (CEDEN, TX); fewer low birthweight babies and increased use of prenatal care (Resource Mothers, SC); fewer low birthweight babies (Parents Too Soon and Ounce of Prevention, IL). (U.S. GAO, 1990) |

* The Institute of Medicine calculates that $3.50 is saved in medical costs during the first year of life for every dollar spent on reducing the low birth rate by two-and-a-half percentage points, an achievement substantially exceeded by all three prenatal care programs described here (Institute of Medicine, 1985).

applying judgment and intelligence to understanding the relationships among diverse findings, it is possible to identify programs that work and to search out the elements that seem to account for their effectiveness.

## ATTRIBUTES OF EFFECTIVE SERVICES

Successful programs vary in many particulars, depending on their domain and auspices and in response to the needs of the populations they serve. But they seem consistently to share a number of common attributes.

Schorr (1988) described the operation of some 17 programs in the fields of family planning, prenatal care, child health, child welfare/family support, child care and preschool education, and elementary school education that had shown evidence of reducing rates of damaging outcomes in adolescence or their antecedent risk factors among disadvantaged children. These programs were examined for the factors that seemed to account for program effectiveness, and a number of common attributes were identified.

It now seems timely to revisit the conclusions drawn almost three years ago and to refine and expand them in the light of subsequent findings from the same and other domains.

To arrive at an updated set of essential attributes of effective programs, I have reviewed my own earlier findings, as well as the findings of others who have reviewed successful programs for young children in health, child care, preschool and elementary education, mental health, and social services. I have also incorporated findings from studies of effective schools, job training programs, programs for teenage mothers, and other interventions aimed primarily at adolescents and young adults, to the extent that they shed light on overarching characteristics of effective services. (I have made no attempt to include findings particular to only a single domain—e.g., staff/child ratios in preschool programs.) The appendix lists the sources on which the following set of attributes are based.

There is evidence of a growing consensus—especially among practitioners—that the following points constitute the major essential attributes of effective programs for disadvantaged children and families. Although there may be some disagreement around the details of the individual attributes, when they are seen in their totality, a clear picture of policy and program implications emerges.

*Successful programs are comprehensive, flexible, and responsive.* They take responsibility for providing easy and coherent access to services that are sufficiently extensive and intensive to meet the major needs of those they work with. They overcome fragmentation through staff versatility, flexibility, and by active collaboration across bureaucratic and professional boundaries.

In the interests of providing continuity and a rich, comprehensive mix of services, these programs put previously disparate services together and add missing pieces by breaking down or crossing traditional barriers in ingenious and innovative ways. In responding to a wide range of needs, these programs do not, in fact, provide everything to everyone, but all offer more than a single category of service or support.

The effective prenatal care program may not itself provide housing assistance or drug treatment, but neither does it ignore the impending eviction or the sudden revelation of a drug problem by one of its patients. A Homebuilders therapist may help an overwhelmed mother to clean her kitchen, or the elementary school principal may add a washing machine to her office equipment.

It is the unrigid, responsive stance of individual staff and of the program or institution as a whole that is characteristic, the fact that no one says,

"This may be what you need, but helping you get it is not part of my job or outside our jurisdiction" (Schorr, 1988). While always keeping their primary mission in mind, staff seem to be forever willing to "push the boundaries of their job description" (Bane, 1990) or to take on an "extended role" in the lives of their students (or patients or clients) (Whelage, 1989). They seem not to give up even when progress is slow or unsteady.

*Successful programs deal with the child as an individual and as part of a family and with the family as part of a neighborhood and community.* Most successful programs have deep roots in the community and respond to needs perceived and identified by the community. They collaborate with parents and local communities to create programs and institutions that respond to unique needs of many different kinds of populations.

Successful programs are not imposed from without, they are not "parachuted" into communities but are carefully and collaboratively integrated with local community needs, resources, and strengths (Council of State Policy and Planning Agencies, 1990). They tend to be explicit about taking a developmental approach, recognizing the stages of the family life-cycle and of child development. Most take a two-generational approach, responding simultaneously to the needs of children and their families.

In the Comer schools in New Haven, as well as in many Head Start programs, parents become long-term supporters of their children's education as their own needs are recognized and met. Successful programs respond to the immediate needs of an individual child, but they do not stop there. The clinician treating an infant for recurrent diarrhea sees beyond the patient on the examining table to whether the family needs a source of clean water or help from a public health nurse or social worker to obtain nonmedical services.

*Staff in successful programs have the time, training, skills, and institutional support necessary to create an accepting environment and to build relationships of trust and respect with children and families.* They work in settings that allow them to develop meaningful one-to-one relationships and to provide services respectfully, ungrudgingly, and collaboratively.

Staff of these programs tend to be well-qualified, highly motivated, and to possess relevant life experience. The "centrality of human relationships" (Lightfoot, 1989) and the creation of "a warm, supportive environment" (Weiss, 1988) is repeatedly stressed when program staff are asked to reflect on program effectiveness, as is the need to draw disadvantaged populations into "a sense of membership in the community" (Whelage, 1989) by reducing the size of the institution and emphasizing intensive, personal, caring, face-to-face relationships with responsible adults in many varied settings. Front-line workers in these programs are provided with the same respect, nurturing, and support by program managers that they are expected to extend to those they serve (Bruner, 1990).

*Programs that are successful with the most disadvantaged populations persevere in their efforts to reach the hardest-to-reach and tailor their services to respond to the distinctive needs of those at greatest risk.*

The attributes described above seem to be most crucial to success in dealing with the most disadvantaged. Whether they work exclusively with high-risk individuals and families or a more heterogeneous population, successful programs report that for those at highest risk, individualized services must be *more individualized*, intensive services must be made yet *more intensive*, and comprehensive services must be made yet *more comprehensive*.

For example, the components of conventional obstetrical medicine fall short of meeting the needs of pregnant women at multiple risk. A pregnant teenager who is depressed, frightened, not eating properly, using drugs or alcohol, and without a permanent home needs a great deal more than medical care if she is to have a healthy baby and get the help she needs in preparing to care for her new child.

Similarly, for the most disadvantaged young people, remedial education and skills training are most effective if delivered in a residential, intensive, highly structured environment, such as offered by the Job Corps (Hahn and Lerman, 1985).

Many of the programs working with multiply disadvantaged children and families see them as very disconnected from the supports traditionally provided by families. They have come to believe that, if they are to effectively perform their formal functions of providing health, education, or social services, these services must be provided in a style similar to that with which families have traditionally responded.

*Successful programs are well-managed, usually by highly competent, energetic, committed, and responsible individuals with clearly identifiable skills and attitudes.*

These managers define and adhere to clear goals and missions but provide for great flexibility in day-to-day operations and allow the program to evolve over time in order to maintain its responsiveness to individual, family, and community needs.

Considering how widespread is the belief that behind every successful program is a leader of such charismatic power that there are no more than a handful of such magical persons to be found in the land, it is significant that Olivia Golden of the Kennedy School at Harvard University has identified a number of distinctive (but nonmagical) attributes possessed by managers of effective programs (Golden, 1988, 1989). These include a willingness:

• to experiment and take risks,
• to manage by "groping along," as the program continually evolves in response to changing needs,

• to tolerate ambiguity,

• to win the trust simultaneously of line workers, politicians, and the public, with a powerful focus on agency mission and careful attention to politically risky decisions,

• to respond to demands for prompt, tangible evidence of improved outcomes,

• to recruit, select, and supervise staff collaboratively and to allow staff to make flexible, individualized decisions.

In short, these program managers have been able to use identifiable management techniques to create a new organizational culture, which is less rule-bound and more outcome-oriented than most traditional agencies, institutions, and systems. They create supportive settings that are stable enough to permit staff to learn from their own mistakes and to draw on a broad base of experience and research in keeping the program responsive to changing needs.

*Successful programs have common theoretical foundations that undergird their client-centered and preventive orientation.*

Client (or patient or student) needs seem to guide the program more powerfully than the imperatives of the institutions and systems within which they operate. Staff of these programs clearly believe in what they are doing. Those in programs that intervene in the early years are convinced of the power of early intervention. Those that work with adolescents and young adults are convinced that "it's never too late to help."

Successful programs seek to replace the prevailing preoccupation with failure and crisis with an orientation that is long-term, preventive, and empowering. First-graders in the Baltimore schools' Success for All program are given "whatever help they need" to acquire basic reading-related skills before they begin to fail and to fall behind (Madden et. al., 1988). Even programs like Homebuilders, whose intervention is triggered by a crisis, focus on long-term change and on helping families to better control their own lives. Most successful programs have very concrete interim goals, but they see their purpose as helping to alter life trajectories over the long term.

## POLICY IMPLICATIONS OF THE ESSENTIAL ATTRIBUTES OF EFFECTIVE SERVICES

Our doubts are traitors and make us lose the good we oft might win, by fearing to attempt.

— William Shakespeare

Perhaps the most striking conclusion that emerges from looking at these characteristics of effective programs is how different they are from most prevailing programs. As Mary Jo Bane points out, "The key to the success of these programs lies in the quality of interactions that go on between individual service providers and clients. These interactions tend to be situation specific and immediately responsive, like the interactions that go on in effective families or classrooms. They tend to be performed by relatively autonomous professionals who exercise a fair amount of discretion in responding to needs" (Bane, 1990).

Some observers conclude that programs that incorporate these attributes could never be made available to large numbers, because programs with these attributes are difficult to replicate and tend to exist primarily outside or at the margins of large human service systems. With the notable exception of the Head Start program initiated as part of the War on Poverty and the efforts to institutionalize family preservation and certain aspects of school reform, a policy thrust to undertake systematic social change to make these unusual attributes the norm has not been seriously considered among developers of social policy. In fact, a quite contrary view is typical. For example, the 1988 Office of Technology Assessment report, *Healthy Children*, concludes its review of effective nurse home visiting programs by noting that these programs are "run by dedicated, enthusiastic, and particularly skilled people, *so it is premature to conclude that the home visitor approach should be broadly applied*" (emphasis added) (Office of Technology Assessment, 1988).

There is no doubt that the major attributes of effective services are fundamentally at odds with the dominant ways that most large institutions and systems are funded and the ways they are expected to assure accountability, quality, and equity:

- Comprehensiveness is at odds with categorical funding.
- Flexibility and front-line worker discretion are at odds with traditional training of professionals and managers and conventional approaches to ensuring accountability through standardizing program operations.
- Intensiveness and individualization are at odds with pressures to ensure equity despite insufficient funds.
- A long-term, preventive orientation is at odds with pressures for immediate payoffs.
- The program's ability to evolve over time is at odds with the pervasiveness of short-term and often unpredictable funding.

Unless the American public is prepared to write off that part of the population that is not going to be effectively helped in the absence of programs that are intensive, comprehensive, family centered, community-grounded, etc., we must begin to engage in systematic exploration of how these prevailing practices might be changed. The challenge is large: essentially to introduce a new culture into human service systems and into major government bureaucracies. Harvard political scientist Steven Kelman writes of this effort in a somewhat broader context as involving the essential "renewal of the public sector" (Kelman, 1990). Nothing less is implied by current findings regarding the attributes of effective programs.

The design of strategies aimed at the wider implementation of effective programs for disadvantaged children and their families must take account, therefore, of the following seven propositions:

1. *If effective services are to reach far larger numbers, information about the essential common attributes of successful programs must be widely disseminated and accompanied by information about strategies to overcome the major impediments to implementing programs with these attributes.*

We have operated too long on the assumption that program success alone will guarantee long-term survival and growth. In the absence of supportive and responsive systems, successful programs do not contain the seeds of their own replication because they do not create systems change. Even the dissemination of information about successful models does not result in their replication in the absence of systems change. Local communities have to own and shape local programs, but local communities can't change state and federal regulations or funding incentives; nor can they protect their innovations from bureaucratic pressures that stifle the unusual.

Strategies based on the creation and dissemination of models are less likely to succeed than strategies that combine identifying and disseminating the essential common attributes of successful programs with identifying and reducing the major impediments to implementing effective programs. These impediments include prevailing methods of financing and regulating programs, of holding programs accountable, and of training professionals; policies governing eligibility and targeting; lack of widespread availability of appropriate technical assistance and of continuing information about promising new approaches to encouraging needed systems change; and lack of public understanding of the key issues.

2. *New funding mechanisms must be developed for targeting resources to geographic areas in which poverty and other risk factors are concentrated.*

Successful programs seem to have been able to attract high-risk populations to utilize a range of services, including preventive services, without basing eligibility on proof of individual failure or on identification of individual handicaps. The absence of high-quality services in these areas, despite their desperate need, suggests the utility of targeting resources on distressed neighborhoods, with eligibility based on residence in the area.

One way this could be accomplished is by combining a certain proportion of current expenditures into a flexible funding stream that would support a coherent array of intensive services in these areas. Through the use of automatic waivers and other regulatory or legislative changes, funds from maternal and child health programs, compensatory education, family support, child care, mental health and social services would become a predictable source of support to comprehensive programs targeted on a high-risk population that would be defined geographically. Neighborhood targeting would minimize barriers of access, reduce fragmentation, and impact the powerful neighborhood-level determinants of child and family well-being.

An initiative aimed at modifying public funding practices in this way could be modest in scale without being trivial. It would begin to change lives among the populations at highest risk; simultaneously, such a strategy would generate information about how to grapple with a broad range of systems issues. It would give expression to a public policy that would get away from making eligibility for services contingent on individual proof of failure, but would recognize that whole communities may be so depleted that a critical mass of new sources of opportunity and support will be required if ordinary youngsters are to succeed in climbing out of poverty and despair. Where systems have failed whole communities in the past, change probably must achieve a visible, critical mass to have a significant impact and to inspire confidence in both clients and program staff that this time change is real and here to stay. A neighborhood focus would make it possible to achieve such a critical mass with substantially less money than would be required by programs that would also extend to less needy populations.

3. *Systematic efforts are needed to bring about a major shift toward the use of outcome measurement to ensure accountability in social programs.*

It is unlikely that the programs that are essential to changing outcomes for disadvantaged youngsters will receive adequate funds under more flexible conditions in the absence of their ability to document their effectiveness in improved real-world outcomes.

An enhanced capacity to measure outcomes would move the discussion about both policies and programs to a focus on changes in the lives of people. By shifting accountability from a reliance on rigid rules and on documenting processes to a reliance on substantive results, human service programs could more easily adopt the attributes of effective programs (see Kelman, 1987, 1990; Hornbeck, in this volume; Gardner, 1989).

It will require a great deal of sustained and thoughtful work to develop the critical outcome indicators that would allow informed judgments of whether a program is in fact accomplishing its intended purpose. Outcome measures must be designed carefully, so they will not become instruments of program corruption or distortion. But it seems more consistent with what we have learned about successful programs to engage in this struggle, than to continue past practices that put a premium on blind adherence to rules at the expense of accomplishing the program's purposes. A shift toward reliance on outcome measures would encourage "the wise exercise of discretion, judgment, and creativity to achieve agreed upon ends" (Kelman, 1990) that characterizes effective programs.

4. *New training mechanisms must be developed, and existing training mechanisms must be modified to enable more individuals to function as competent front-line workers or managers in effective programs.*

As we have seen, front-line workers as well as program managers in successful programs exhibit skills and attitudes that do not seem to be the products of conventional professional training. Obviously their ability to build trusting, collaborative relationships, to work flexibly and to cross disciplinary and professional boundaries, to exercise front-line discretion and to address a complex interplay of problems, as well as the ability of managers to utilize distinctive skills—all these are not solely the product of *training.* But the creation of new training capacity would increase the numbers of skilled individuals that could function inorganizations that incorporate and create these expectations and who could comfortably adopt an expanded definition of what it means to act like a professional. The availability of high- quality professional training could also help to make work in effective programs attractive to a new pool of talented, eager, and committed individuals.

5. *States, communities, and local agencies will need competent technical assistance, both in program development and in their efforts to change policies and practices to better reflect the lessons of successful programs.*

Organizations that seek to improve outcomes for disadvantaged children need more than information about successful programs to put such programs in place. Many communities may recognize the need for change but don't know how to get started on making change happen. States that expect to reform their policies and practices to create more supportive settings for effective programs will need highly skilled, knowledgeable, and individualized technical assistance.

6. *Continuing efforts are needed to build the magnitude of public understanding that will support needed action.*

The needed political support necessary to attack today's most urgent domestic problems is unlikely to materialize unless the following concepts become part of the general understanding of a majority of Americans.

• The most serious problems of disadvantaged children, youth, and families are inextricably bound up with structural changes in the American society and economy that are far more powerful than the changes that can be made by individuals and families through their own talents and efforts.

• Society's stake in investing in promising solutions is so great that continuing failure to undertake promising or proven programs of intervention and support will be destructive of the national interest.

• The elements of many promising solutions are now reasonably well known, and the widespread implementation of effective interventions requires fundamental systems changes.

• Effective interventions are a cost-effective investment even when they require substantial initial funding.

• There are no quick, cheap fixes. A long-term view is essential, for the impact of effective services or their absence must be seen intergenerationally. The long-term needs of the next generation must not be sacrificed in order to achieve short-term savings in this generation. The results of effective interventions are worth waiting for, even though they can rarely be documented during a single budget cycle or during the term of office of their political champion.

7. *The time is ripe for systematic action to promote systems change.*

Efforts currently under way in many states and communities to improve services to disadvantaged children and their families are hampered by the absence of strategic thinking, clear leadership, and shared relevant information. Exploration of how this need might best be met is now timely. Among the functions that are not now being performed in an integrated fashion, that might usefully be performed by one or more organizations (existing or newly formed for this purpose, are the following:

• To be a source of reliable and up-to-date information regarding the attributes of effective programs and the attributes of effective or promising systems change. This would entail the capacity to perform continuing assessments of current efforts in program and policy development and implementation, to determine whether there are common patterns thatcharacterize the most promising efforts, and to identify the most successful strategies for overcoming major obstacles and to communicate widely findings regarding both effective and ineffective efforts. In an analog to the Manpower Demonstration and Research Corporation, this function could include the capacity to fund and evaluate a coordinated series of demonstrations of neighborhood-wide or community-wide funding and delivery of comprehensive, effective services.

• To provide opportunities for joint learning and problem solving around such issues as financing, training, technical assistance, governance, accountability, and evaluation.

• To encourage and assist in the development and utilization of well-designed outcome measures; to encourage the widespread use of evaluation approaches that take into account the distinctive attributes of interventions that are most likely to be effective among disadvantaged populations.

• To encourage coordinated action to overcome these barriers to "going-to-scale" that successful programs are least likely to be able to overcome through local action alone.

• To be a source of leadership in efforts to educate the public on the major issues relevant to bringing about the changes needed to improve services for disadvantaged children and their families.

## CONCLUSION

Policies and programs significantly different from those that prevail are known to improve the odds for children growing up in family and neighborhood environments that do not provide them with the protection, nurturance, and social capital they need to succeed in school and in life. Most local programs operate with a funding base, and in a political, bureaucratic, and professional context that makes it nearly impossible to provide the multifaceted responses that could change outcomes for families with multiple, complex needs.

To reach a high proportion of the children at greatest risk with the interventions and supports that will improve their futures requires fundamental transformation of both localprograms and the policies that shape them. But the levers of change that have been available until now are not sufficiently connected to one another and are not strong or far-reaching enough to bring about needed changes in the systems within which most programs operate.

Much activity and random experimentation is currently under way in local communities and states all around the nation aimed at improving the circumstances of disadvantaged children, but to little discernible long-range effect. The widespread yearning to do better could, however, be transformed into effective action. The deliberations of this workshop provide an extraordinary opportunity to identify the strategies that could arm government officials, business leaders, practitioners, program managers, philanthropists, and concerned citizens with the tools they need to bring about systematic change on a scale that has a reasonable relationship to the magnitude of the need, and therefore a reasonable chance to succeed.

## REFERENCES

Bane, Mary Jo
    1990   Paying Attention to Children Services, Settings and Systems. Paper prepared for the Workshop on Effective Services for Young Children, November 1-2, Washington, D.C.

Bane, Mary Jo, and David T. Ellwood
    1989   One fifth of the nation's children: Why are they poor? *Science* 245:1047-53.

Berrueta-Clement, J.R., L.J. Schweinhart, W.S. Barnett, A.E. Epstein, and D.P. Weikart
    1984   *Changed Lives: The Effects of the Perry Preschool Programs on Youths Through Age 19.* Ypsilanti, Michigan: High/Scope Press.

Comer, J.P.
    1985   The Yale-New Haven Primary Prevention Project: A follow-up study. *Journal of the American Academy of Child Psychiatry* 24(2):154-60.
    1988   Educating poor minority children. *Scientific American* 259(5):42-48.

Congress of the United States
  1988  *Healthy Children: Investing in the Future.* Office of Technology Assessment.
Deutsch, M., C.P. Deutsch, T.J. Jordan, and R. Grallo
  1983  The IDS Program: An experiment in early and sustained enrichment. Pp. 377-410
        in *As the Twig Is Bent . . . Lasting Effects of Preschool Programs.* Consortium for
        Longitudinal Studies. Hillsdale, N.J.: Lawrence Erlbaum Associates.
Danziger, Sheldon, and Jonathan Stern
  1990  The Causes and Consequences of Child Poverty in the United States. Paper pre-
        pared for UNICEF, International Child Development Center, Project on Child Pov-
        erty and Deprivation in Industrialized Countries.
Edwards, L.E., M.E. Steinman, and E.Y. Hakanson
  1977  An experimental comprehensive high school clinic. *American Journal of Public
        Health* 8:765-76.
Edwards, L.E., M.E. Steinman, K. Arnold, and E.Y. Hakanson
  1980  Adolescent pregnancy prevention services in high school clinics. *Family Planning
        Perspectives* 12(1):6-14.
Edna McConnell Clark Foundation
  1985  *Keeping Families Together: The Case for Family Preservation.* New York: Edna
        McConnell Clark Foundation.
Furstenberg, Frank F., Jr., J. Brooks-Gunn, and S. Philip Morgan
  1987  *Adolescent Mothers in Later Life.* Cambridge: Cambridge University Press.
Gardner, Sid
  1989  Failure by Fragmentation. *California Tomorrow* Pp. 18-25.
Grant Foundation Commission
  1988  The Forgotten Half: Pathways to Success for America's Youth and Young Families.
        Final Report, Youth and America's Future.
Gray, S.W., B.K. Ramsey, and R.A. Klaus
  1983  The Early Training Project 1962-1980. Pp. 33-69 in *As the Twig Is Bent . . . Lasting
        Effects of Preschool Programs.* Consortium for Longitudinal Studies. Hillsdale,
        N.J.: Lawrence Erlbaum Associates.
Golden, Olivia
  1988  Balancing Entrepreneurship, Line Worker Discretion, and Political Accountability:
        The Delicate Task of Innovators in Human Services. Paper presented to the 1988
        Annual Meeting of the Association for Public Policy Analysis and Management,
        Seattle, Washington, October 27-29.
  1989  Innovation in Public Sector Human Service Programs: The Implications of Innova-
        tion by 'Groping Along.'" Unpublished paper.
Hahn, Andrew, and Robert Lerman
  1985  *What Works in Youth Employment Policy?* Report #3. Washington, D.C.: National
        Planning Association.
Hardy, J.
  1981  A comprehensive approach to adolescent pregnancy. In K.G. Scott, T. Field, and E.
        Robertson, eds., *Teenage Parents and Their Offsprings.* New York: Grune & Stratton.
Harvard Family Research Project
  1990  *Innovative Models to Guide Family Support and Education Policy in the 1990s: An
        Analysis of Four Pioneering State Programs.* Cambridge: Harvard Graduate School
        of Education.
The Infant Health and Development Program
        Enhancing the outcomes of low-birth-weight, premature infants: A multisite, ran-
        domized trial. *Journal of the American Medical Association* 263:3035-3042.
Institute of Medicine
  1985  *Preventing Low Birthweight.* Committee to Study the Prevention of Low Birthweight,

Division of Health Promotion and Disease Prevention. Washington, D.C.: National Academy Press.

Kelman, Steven
1987 *Making Public Policy: A Hopeful View of American Government.* Basic Books, Inc.: New York.
1990 The renewal of the public sector. *The American Prospect* 51-8.

Kinney, J.M., B. Madsen, T. Fleming, and D.A. Haapala
1977 Homebuilders: keeping families together. *Journal of Consulting and Clinical Psychology* 45(4):667-73.

Korenbrot, C.C.
1984 Risk reduction in pregnancies of low income women: comprehensive prenatal care through the OB access project. *Mobius* 4:34-43.

Lazar, I., R.B. Darlington, H. Murray, J. Royce, and A. Snipper
1982 *Lasting Effects of Early Education.* Monographs of the Society for Research in Child Development. Vol. 47.

Lightfoot, Sara Lawrence
1989 Visions of a Better Way: A Black Appraisal of Public Schooling. Report of the Committee on Policy for Racial Justice, Joint Center for Political Studies.

McLanahan, S.
1988 Family structure and dependency: Early transitions to female household headship. *Demography* 25(1).

Madden, Nancy A., R.E. Slavin, N.L. Karweit, B.J. Livermon, and L. Dolan
1988 Success for All: First-Year Effects of a Comprehensive Plan for Reforming Urban Education. Paper presented at the annual conference of the American Educational Research Association, San Francisco. Center for Research on Elementary and Middle Schools, Johns Hopkins University.

National Center for Children in Poverty
1990 *Five Million Children: A Statistical Profile of Our Poorest Young Citizens.* New York: School of Public Health, Columbia University.

Nothdurft, William E. with Barbara Dyer
1990 *Out from Under: Policy Lessons from a Quarter Century of Wars on Poverty.* Based on field research by Alan Okagaki in cooperation with the Corporation for Enterprise Development. Washington, D.C.: The Council of State Policy and Planning Agencies.

Olds, D.L., C.R. Henderson, R. Tatelbaum, and R. Chamberlin
1986 Improving the delivery of prenatal care and outcomes of pregnancy: A randomized trial of nurse home visitation. *Pediatrics* 77(1):16-28.

Peters, Thomas J. and Robert H. Waterman, Jr.
1982 *In Search of Excellence.* New York: Warner Books.

Plotnick, R.
1987 Welfare and Other Determinants of Teenage Out-of-Wedlock Childbearing. Paper presented to Research Conference of the Association for Public Policy Analysis and Management.

Schorr, Lisbeth B., with Daniel Schorr
1988 *Within Our Reach: Breaking the Cycle of Disadvantage.* New York: Doubleday/ Anchor Press.

Seitz, Y., L.K. Rosenbaum, and N.H. Apfel
1985 Effects of family support intervention: A ten-year follow-up. *Child Development* 53:376-91.

Unger, D.G., and L.P. Wandersman
1985 Social support and adolescent mothers: Action research contributions to theory and application. *Journal of Social Issues* 41(1):29-45.

U.S. General Accounting Office
1990 Home Visiting: A Promising Early Intervention Strategy for At-Risk Families. Report to the Chairman, Subcommittee on Labor, Health and Human Services, Education, and Related Agencies, Committee on Appropriations, U.S. Senate.
Wilson, William Julius
1987 *The Truly Disadvantaged: The Inner City, the Underclass, and Public Policy.* Chicago: University of Chicago Press.
Zabin, L.S., M.B. Hirsch, E.A. Smith, R. Streett, and J.B. Hardy
1986 Evaluation of a pregnancy prevention program for urban teenagers. *Family Planning Perspectives* 18(3):119-26.

## APPENDIX

Adolescent Pregnancy Prevention Clearinghouse
1989 *The Lessons of Multi-Site Initiatives Serving High-Risk Youths.* Washington, D.C.: Children's Defense Fund.
Berrueta-Clement, J.R., L.J. Schweinhart, W.S. Barnett, A.E. Epstein, and D.P. Weikart
1984 *Changed Lives: The Effects of the Perry Preschool Programs on Youths Through Age 19.* Ypsilanti, Michigan: High/Scope Press.
Burghardt, John, and A. Gordon
1990 *More Jobs and Higher Pay: How an Integrated Program Compares with Traditional Programs.* New York: Rockefeller Foundation.
Charney, E.
1984 Preparing physicians in training for child health care communication. Pp. 203-16 in W.K. Frankenburg and S.M. Thornton, eds., *Child Health Care Communications.* The Johnson and Johnson Pediatric Round Table VIII. New York: Praeger.
Comer, J.P.
1980 *School Power.* New York: Free Press.
1984 Home-school relationships as they affect the academic success of children. *Education and Urban Society* 16(3):323-37.
1985 The Yale-New Haven Primary Prevention Project: A follow-up study. *Journal of the American Academy of Child Psychiatry* 24(2):154-60.
1987 *Children in Need: Investment Strategies for the Educationally Disadvantaged.* New York: Committee for Economic Development.
1988 Educating poor minority children. *Scientific American* 259(5):42-48.
Consortium for Longitudinal Studies
1983 *As the Twig Is Bent . . . Lasting Effects of Preschool Programs.* Hillsdale, N.J.: Lawrence Erlbaum Associates.
Cuban, L.
1984 Transforming the frog into a prince: Effective schools research, policy and practice at the district level. *Harvard Educational Review* 54(2):129-51.
Deutsch, M., C.P. Deutsch, T.J. Jordan, and R. Grallo
1983 The IDS Program: An experiment in early and sustained enrichment. Pp. 377-410 in Consortium for Longitudinal Studies, *As the Twig Is Bent . . . Lasting Effects of Preschool Programs.* Hillsdale, N.J.: Lawrence Erlbaum Associates.
Dryfoos, Joy G.
1990 *Adolescents at Risk.* New York: Oxford University Press.
Community schools: New institutional arrangements for preventing high-risk behavior. *FLEducator* 4-9.
Edmonds, R.
1979 Effective schools for the urban poor. *Educational Leadership* 15-27.

Edna McConnell Clark Foundation
  1985 *Keeping Families Together: The Case for Family Preservation.* New York: Edna McConnell Clark Foundation.
Edwards, L.E., M.E. Steinman, and E.Y. Hakanson
  1977 An experimental comprehensive high school clinic. *American Journal of Public Health* 8:765-76.
Edwards, L.E., M.E. Steinman, K. Arnold, and E.Y. Hakanson
  1980 Adolescent pregnancy prevention services in high school clinics. *Family Planning Perspectives* 12(1):6-14.
Ford Foundation
  1989 *Early Childhood Services: A National Challenge.* New York: Ford Foundation.
Golden, Olivia
  1988 Balancing Entrepreneurship, Line Worker Discretion, and Political Accountability: The Delicate Task of Innovators in Human Services. Paper presented to the 1988 Annual Meeting of the Association for Public Policy Analysis and Management, Seattle, Washington, October 27-29.
  1989 Innovation in Public Sector Human Service Programs: The Implications of Innovation by "Groping Along." Unpublished paper.
Gray, S.W., B.K. Ramsey, and R.A. Klaus
  1983 The Early Training Project 1962-1980. Pp. 33-69 in Consortium for Longitudinal Studies, *As the Twig Is Bent . . . Lasting Effects of Preschool Programs.* Hillsdale, N.J.: Lawrence Erlbaum Associates.
Hahn, Andrew, and Robert Lerman
  1985 *What Works in Youth Employment Policy?* Report #3. Washington, D.C.: National Planning Association.
Halpern, Robert and Heather Weiss
  1989 Family Support and Education Programs. Paper prepared for the Public Policy and Family Support and Education Programs Colloquium, April 26-28.
Hardy, J.
  1981 A comprehensive approach to adolescent pregnancy. In K.G. Scott, T. Field, and E. Robertson, eds., *Teenage Parents and Their Offsprings.* New York: Grune & Stratton.
Harvard Family Research Project
  1990 Innovative Models to Guide Family Support and Education Policy in the 1990s. Unpublished paper.
Hershey, Alan
  1988 *The Minority Female Single Parent Demonstration: Program Operations.* A Technical Research Report. New York: The Rockefeller Foundation.
Hollister, Robinson, G., Jr.
  1990 *New Evidence About Effective Training Strategies.* New York: The Rockefeller Foundation.
Kinney, J.M., B. Madsen, T. Fleming, and D.A. Haapala
  1977 Homebuilders: Keeping families together. *Journal of Consulting and Clinical Psychology* 45(4):667-73.
Korenbrot, C.C.
  1984 Risk reduction in pregnancies of low income women: Comprehensive prenatal care through the OB access project. *Mobius* 4:34-43.
Lazar, I., R.B. Darlington, H. Murray, J. Royce, and A. Snipper
  1982 *Lasting Effects of Early Education.* Monographs of the Society for Research in Child Development. Vol. 47.
Lightfoot, Sara Lawrence
  1989 Visions of a Better Way: A Black Appraisal of Public Schooling. Report of the Committee on Policy for Racial Justice, Joint Center for Political Studies.

Madden, Nancy A., R.E. Slavin, N.L. Karweit, B.J. Livermon, and L. Dolan
  1988  Success for All: First-Year Effects of a Comprehensive Plan for Reforming Urban Education. Paper presented at the annual conference of the American Educational Research Association, San Francisco. Center for Research on Elementary and Middle Schools, Johns Hopkins University.
Miller, Jerome
  1989  Is rehabilitation a waste of time? *The Washington Post* (Outlook section), April 23.
Ministry of Community and Social Services, Ontario
  1989  *Better Beginnings, Better Futures: An Integrated Model of Primary Prevention of Emotional and Behavioural Problems.* Queen's Printer for Ontario. ISBN0-772-96148-4.
Olds, D.L., C.R. Henderson, R. Chamberlin, and R. Tatelbaum
  1986  Preventing child abuse and neglect: A randomized trial of nurse home visitation. *Pediatrics* 78:65-78.
Olds, D.L., C.R. Henderson, R. Tatelbaum, and R. Chamberlin
  1986  Improving the delivery of prenatal care and outcomes of pregnancy: A randomized trial of nurse home visitation. *Pediatrics* 77(1):16-28.
Olds, David L., and Harriet Kitzman
  1990  Can home visitation improve the health of women and children at environmental risk? *Pediatrics* 86(1):108-116.
Pierson, D.E., D.K. Walker, and T. Tivnan
  1984  A school-based program from infancy to kindergarten for children and their parents. *Personnel and Guidance Journal* 62(8):448-55.
Price, Richard H.
  1987  What Do Successful Programs Have in Common? Testimony given to the House Select Committee on Children, Youth and Families, April 28. Task Force on Promotion, Prevention and Intervention Alternatives of the American Psychological Association.
Price, Richard H., E.L. Cowen, R.P. Lorion, J. Ramos-McKay
  1989  The search for effective prevention programs: What we learned along the way. *American Orthopsychiatric Association, Inc.* 59(1):49-58.
Provence, S., and A. Naylor
  1983  *Working with Disadvantaged Parents and Their Children.* New Haven: Yale University Press.
Purkcy, S.C., and M.S. Smith
  1983  Effective schools: A review. *Elementary School Journal* 83(4):427-52.
Rutter, M., B. Maughan, P. Mortimore, and J. Ouston
  1979  *Fifteen Thousand Hours: Secondary Schools and Their Effects on Children.* Cambridge, Mass.: Harvard University Press.
Schorr, Lisbeth B., with D. Schorr
  1988  *Within Our Reach: Breaking the Cycle of Disadvantage.* New York: Doubleday/Anchor Press.
Schweinhart, L.J., and D.P. Weikart
  1983  The effects of the Perry Preschool Program on Youths through age 15. Pp.71-101 in Consortium for Longitudinal Studies, *As the Twig Is Bent . . . Lasting Effects of Preschool Programs.* Hillsdale, N.J.: Lawrence Bribaum Associates.
Seitz, Y., L.K. Rosenbaum, and N.H. Apfel
  1985  Effects of family support intervention: A ten-year follow-up. *Child Development* 53:376-91.
Shipman, V.C.
  1976  *Disadvantaged Children and Their First School Experiences.* Princeton, N.J.: Educational Testing Service.

Tyack, D., and E. Hansor
  1982 Hard times, hard choices: The case for coherence in public school leadership. *Phi Delta Kappan*: 511-515.
Unger, D.G., and L.P. Wandersman
  1985 Social support and adolescent mothers: Action research contributions to theory and application. *Journal of Social Issues* 41(1):29-45.
U.S. Congress
  1989 *Healthy Children: Investing in the Future.* 12th Congress, Office of Technology Assessment, OTA-H-345. Washington, D.C.: U.S. Government Printing Office.
U.S. Public Health Service
  1989 *Caring for Our Future: The Content of Prenatal Care.* Washington, D.C.: U.S. Department of Health and Human Services.
Weikart, David P.
  1989 *Quality Preschool Programs: A Long-Term Social Investment.* Occasional Paper Number Five, Ford Foundation Project on Social Welfare and the American Future. New York: Ford Foundation.
Whelage, Gary G.
  1989 *Reducing the Risk: Schools as Communities of Support.* New York: Falmer Press.
Whittaker, James K., J. Kinney, E.M. Tracy, and C. Booth, eds.
  1990 *Reaching High-Risk Families: Intensive Family Preservation in Human Services.* Aldine de Gruyter.
Zabin, L.S., M.B. Hirsch, E.A. Smith, R. Streett, and J.B. Hurdy.
  1986 Evaluation of a pregnancy prevention program for urban teenagers. *Family Planning Perspectives* 18(3):119-26.
Zigler, E., and J. Valentino, eds.
  1979 *Project Head Start: A Legacy of the War on Poverty.* New York: Free Press.

# Effective Services for Children and Families: Lessons from the Past and Strategies for the Future

*Peter B. Edelman*
Georgetown University Law Center
and
*Beryl A. Radin*
Washington Public Affairs Center
University of Southern California

For three decades Americans have debated the difficult question of how to structure human service delivery systems. Despite the dramatic political, economic, and social changes that have taken place in the United States over the past 30 years, this question has continued to plague social policy analysts and advocates. A number of factors coalesced in the 1960s to define the problems in terms that are with us today.

Thirty years ago a national interest in assisting the poor and minorities with services funded by tax dollars appeared for the first time in a noncrisis context. These efforts combined with the programs of the New Deal to create a social program fabric that was not dissimilar to that of some of the European welfare states. The agreed-upon clientele for services expanded, and the federal government came into the picture as a significant ongoing funding source. The recognized agenda of needs broadened as well. Problems previously ignored became legitimate targets to be addressed. The nation discovered that the poor had legal problems, health problems, and family problems of which it had previously been unaware. Many assumed that the crazy quilt of human services that emerged reflected an acceptance of an active and innovative role at the federal level that, they thought, would in turn bring about rationalization in a coordinated system as time went on.

Questions arose in rapid-fire order about the performance of virtually everyone who had some role in the past. Government at all levels was suspect: old-line federal agencies and states and local governments across the board. State governments were seen as especially moribund. Professionals of all kinds came under attack, from social workers to teachers, doctors, lawyers, and bureaucrats. Institutions, particularly residential ones, that were supposed to deliver services were targets, too, whether they were mental hospitals, schools for the retarded, acute-care hospitals, or jails or even educational institutions, corporations, trade unions, churches, or foundations.

Each of these developments—the broadened definition of clients and service needs, the arrival of noncyclically related federal funding, and the questioning of governmental, professional, and institutional performance— played a role in framing the debate over how to deliver services most effectively that has continued on and off ever since.

The questions that were asked in the 1960s have never been fully answered. For the last decade they were seldom even asked. As the 1990s begin, there is some indication that they are back on the table. So it is time to query: What have we learned? What should we do differently if we get the chance to do something?

## THE 1960S: SUCCESSES OR FAILURES?

In many ways, the experiences of the 1960s have become a Rorschach test for the society. People react reflexively to the mention of the 1960s and see what they want to see, for good or ill. Because the debate over this experience is often waged on so many levels, it is difficult to present a balanced picture of its contributions and limitations.

To begin with, the picture for the poor and minorities in the society is improved in many respects over what it was in 1960. Despite the many problems that remain to be solved and complications that have emerged since that time, some things did get better. At the same time, it is not at all clear how well we have institutionalized these changes. We know that millions of people did escape poverty, especially during the period between 1960 and 1973, but current data suggest that the improvements are fragile at best. Much of what was gained during the civil rights revolution is still largely intact, in legal if not in economic terms. Legal services for the poor are recognized as important even if resources for that activity are significantly lower than during the 1960s. While a revolution for the rights of women came into its own, it too has had difficulty dealing with economic rather than legal rights. Health care for the elderly is vastly improved, despite the current attacks on Medicare funding. Health care for the poor, with all its limitations, is better than it used to be. Services for the mentally retarded and the developmentally disabled have been revolutionized, and the disabled in general have come a long way. The society has acknowledged that early childhood development programs for disadvantaged children are important, as is the need for special nutritional attention for low-income pregnant mothers and young children.

These are not trivial advances, and most of them originated in initiatives that began in the 1960s. Despite this, the 1960s have a bad name, even among many sophisticated people. The debate over these issues—particularly over program structures and strategies—is so entangled with other political battles of the period that it evokes great controversy. For some, the scary and even scarring memories of the period are a barrier to fine-tuned discussion. For others, a broadside attack on the period (or a blanket defense, for that matter) is a way of avoiding an extremely difficult policy question: What is the standard that we want to use to evaluate the programs created then? Were they meant to eliminate all problems (as the rhetoric of promises suggested), or were they meant to be incremental changes constituting an acknowledgment that these problems do exist and a commitment to further increments that would over time evolve into a solid system?

Much of the debate over the contribution of the 1960s revolves around the Community Action Program and the Model Cities Program—the two most conceptually radical attempts to deal with service delivery problems. Both attempted to create new structures that would perform planning and coordination functions at the grass-roots level, providing mechanisms to deliver services to the unserved or underserved more effectively than existing institutions.

## Community Action Programs

Under the Community Action Program (CAP), which was a key part of the war on poverty, some 500 community action agencies were set up around the country. CAP was not a program in itself. It was meant to be "a process for mobilizing resources and coordinating other programs," as cited in Freiden and Kaplan, *The Politics of Neglect: Urban Aid from Model Cities to Revenue Sharing* (MIT Press, 1977).

The Economic Opportunity Act created quite a long list of programs: Head Start, Neighborhood Legal Services, Neighborhood Health Centers, Foster Grandparents, Job Corps, VISTA, and various job training programs to be run through the Department of Labor. The idea was that, for those programs that were to be delivered at the local level, the CAP agency would be the umbrella coordinating agency and might run some of the services itself but not necessarily.

This sounds innocuous enough. There were, however, three key features that made the initiative far from innocuous. First, the CAP agencies were set up outside the political system and were not accountable to the mayors or any other local elected or appointed officials. Second, they were to involve the "maximum feasible participation of the poor," which was widely understood to mean that they were to be controlled, in terms of how their boards would be structured, by the people they were intended to serve. Third, their funding came directly from the federal government, not through any intermediate governmental filter.

What happened next was predictable and, it is generally agreed, intended. The CAP agencies began to march on City Hall. They didn't just sue (although they did that, too); they used federal money to rent buses and make signs so they could make demands on city government. They were not beholden to City Hall for anything, and few of them were advised by professionals who might have warned them of the risks of being confrontational. So Mayor Daley of Chicago came to Congress and got Congresswoman Edith Green to amend the law to thwart the CAP agencies' autonomy.

The CAP agencies receded into being small social delivery agencies, basically outside the organized social service delivery system. (That is where many, if not most, of those that survived are today). They still have a small assured source of federal funding via the block grant administered by the Community Services Administration. So they can continue to go it alone if they choose to, although a good number of them have become integrated into local service delivery networks if for no other reason than to get United Way, local foundation, or local government (including Title XX) funding.

Is this a sad story? Absolutely not. Most of the "mini-categorical" programs which the CAP agencies were supposed to coordinate have survived. Some, like Head Start, have made it to the hall of fame of successful social programs. All were transferred to other federal agencies: It is not surprising that parallel programs set up in parallel agencies could not survive in that form. They were conceived as independent efforts so as to escape stultification in a traditional bureaucracy. They were meant to serve as a yardstick against which to measure the performance of existing programs and as a goad to push old-line agencies to do better. This is not a situation that could be expected to last. The programs originally assigned to the Office of Economic Opportunity largely did what they were intended to do in waking up other bureaucracies. This strategy is not something to be done only once in history. It is entirely appropriate to contemplate a cycle of parallel programs in a parallel agency or agencies every generation or so. While the specifics may be different, it may well be time for another such strategic initiative.

The CAP agencies themselves also made a contribution. During their brief heyday they gave a generation of poor people a taste of having a sense of control over their own lives. They did actually contribute to changing the behavior of some elected officials. And they left behind a group of people who were nurtured there, learned how to use the system, and went on to community leadership in many instances.

They also learned how difficult it is to use public money to set up an alternative politics. Using federal money to fund litigation against governments has been controversial and has barely survived. Political advocacy funded with tax dollars is inherently problematic because the targets of advocacy will fight back.

They learned, too, that direct federal funding of a locally untethered set of service delivery agencies runs a particular risk that such agencies will not become part of a local service delivery network. For the long run, local service delivery agencies and entities which are accountable to or connected to local governmental or philanthropic institutions or networks are going to be more effective than those that are not.

## Model Cities Programs

As the Office of Economic Opportunity was getting launched, planners for the new Department of Housing and Urban Development were working on an initiative based on premises somewhat similar to community action. They, too, envisioned a process that would pull together existing categorical programs at the local level to make them more responsive to the needs of the poor. It was widely felt that the urban renewal efforts of the 1950s had failed to help the poor, and in many cases had hurt them by destroying their housing and not providing anything to replace it.

The Task Force planning that turned out to be Model Cities believed that physical renewal was not enough, that housing construction and rehabilitation had to be combined with education, health, and social services. Their report called for a massive housing program, a total approach, and flexibility regarding local building codes, federal bureaucratic rules, and categorical boundaries. It said three principles should govern: concentration of resources, coordination of talent and programs, and mobilization of local leadership. The idea was that, if new money for housing was added to access to existing federal programs in other areas, enough in the way of resources would be available to stimulate a successful local process to coordinate and build linkages among programs.

The bill finally enacted as Model Cities fell far short of what had been recommended. The Vietnam War robbed it of funds; its implementers were not given the authority that had been sought to pull in funds from other departments. The expediters who were to have been installed to package initiatives for each city were not created. And, on top of everything else, what was originally to have been a small number of concentrated demonstrations was dissipated into some 66 cities. Even without the Vietnam War it is doubtful that enough money would have ever flowed anywhere to demonstrate anything. Lacking either the new money or any way to command access to the existing money, there was no glue to cause people at the local level to take the Model Cities planning process seriously.

There is nothing particularly wrong with the original design of Model Cities. The problem is, it was not enacted into law. One possible lesson is that, if there is a desire to demonstrate what can be done in one neighborhood on a concentrated basis, enough resources had better be made available to make a difference. Model Cities is, if nothing else, a lesson in dissipation of limited resources.

By the end of the 1960s, the scars from the decade pulled strategists away from the community level to focus on coordination and planning at the national level. The initiatives of the 1970s were much more modest in scale. In the early 1970s the programs advanced within the Department of Health, Education, and Welfare (HEW) aimed at coordinating the array of categorical programs that had been created over the years. Policy planners believed that by developing opportunities for consolidation at the national level, state and local agencies would be able to rationalize the system and create new structures that were more effective deliverers of services. HEW funded a number of demonstration programs aimed at the integration of services at the local level but was never able to obtain congressional approval for large-scale reform efforts. During the late 1970s, attempts were also made to foster partnerships of city, state, and federal agencies, but they too remained small-scale programs that were eventually replaced by Reagan administration block grants.

## THIRTY YEARS OF EXPERIENCE: THESIS, ANTITHESIS, AND SYNTHESIS

Much of what the society believes about the programs of the 1960s is colored by the way these efforts were portrayed—even caricatured—in the 1980s. The debate about effective services became a polemical contest centered around three issues: the role of the federal government; money as a lever for change; and the search for a panacea solution. Our thinking about each of these issues was clouded by a battle of myths: the efforts of the 1960s were reduced to slogans and replaced by mirrorlike, opposite slogans in the 1980s. We believe that it is time to go beyond these slogans and to create a discussion in the 1990s that addresses the substance of these issues and not simply to rest on the rhetoric. That is our synthesis.

### The Role of the Federal Government

The mythology about the 1960s is that people believed that federal programs alone could solve the country's social problems. Although there was a tendency in many programs of the 1960s to believe that the essential lever for change came from Washington, there were some other efforts that recognized the contribution of other institutional actors. But the lack of experience within the country about these issues (and the relative naivete of program designers) did contribute to a simplistic approach. There is no question that President Johnson did oversell programs. His exaggerated style did lead to an unreasonable increase in people's expectations. When the problems weren't solved (and new problems such as Vietnam and Watergate emerged), some people became disillusioned and turned away from government.

Given this disillusionment, it is not surprising that the mirror-image myth of the 1980s was that the national government is useless in dealing with domestic social problems and thus has no role to play at all in this effort. Rather than governmental action, we were told that the private sector through voluntary action alone is the appropriate institution and mode of intervention. After eight years of Ronald Reagan's antigovernment government (except in defense), we now have George Bush's kinder, gentler version of the same thing.

The synthesis for the 1990s must be that, although government has a role at all levels, even with the full participation of state and local government, it cannot do the job by itself. These problems will not be solved without the participation of all of us, as individuals and as institutions of which we are a part—our churches, our companies, our unions, the United Way. And the people who need help have an obligation too—to take responsibility for themselves to make the maximum use of the help to achieve self-sufficiency.

The particular role that government should play constitutes a key question. The federal government's role is relatively easy, apart from debates over how much money it will put in. Other than Social Security, activities of the Veterans Administration, certain agricultural matters, the federal prisons, and services for the military and their families, the federal government does not deliver services directly. It pays for them, and in recent years it has moved away from extensive use of tiny categorical programs that tie up state and local governments and private providers in multiple reporting, overlapping and even inconsistent regulations, and multiple planning requirements and grant applications. There is still a large debate over the degree and form of regulation that should accompany federal funding, but at least there are far fewer tiny categorical aid programs to cloud the picture.

Even so, the number of funding streams that confront one trying to organize comprehensive or multiple services from a neighborhood or community perspective is overwhelming and raises important questions about the role of state and local government. To what extent can or should there be a coordinating or packaging function, particularly for local government, at either the neighborhood or municipal level? A related question is the "make or buy" issue—the extent to which government, either state or local, should deliver services itself through its own employees, and the extent to which it should contract or use grants to accomplish its purposes.

One theme governing the answers to these questions should be the idea of community. We seem to have lost the idea that a significant social policy aim is embodied in the notion of community, of a social infrastructure that embodies stability and security and shared values. For many today, individual opportunity is nullified because there is no community around them. No matter how strong their family, the street is a jungle with unsavory and often fatal attractions, pressures, and perils. Surely one role of government is to help rediscover and rebuild the sense of community that we have lost in too many places. Pursuit of this theme should guide new service initiatives as well as efforts to deal with the way services are organized.

## Money as the Lever for Change

The 1960s have been portrayed as an era in which people thought that all that was necessary was to throw money at problems and the problems would disappear. While it was true that people during that era had more confidence in the ability of money to evoke institutional change, the resources for this task were never made available even at the level authorized by Congress, let alone at the scale required to make real change. Viewed in the context of the 1990 budget, it is clear that President Johnson was a big talker, but he was in fact not a big spender. The average annual deficit during his presidency was less than $6 billion, and that includes the years of paying for the Vietnam War.

The 1980s counterpoint to this position was that we can solve social problems without any federal money at all. Somehow, magically, a groundswell from the society would create a climate in which all the needed soup kitchens and homeless shelters would emerge, inspired and guided by a lot of tough talk from Washington. If government funds were required, they would come from the local community or from the state.

The 1990s synthesis has to be that we cannot solve the problems without money, but that money alone will not solve the problems. We have to confront deeper structural failings. School bureaucracies are stultified, and principals and teachers are blocked from taking initiatives that would benefit their students. Public housing units in many major cities stand unoccupied for lack of maintenance, not just lack of funds. Our health-care system is still excessively hospital-based and not sufficiently preventive.

That there is a major structural agenda is particularly worth bearing in mind in talking about effective services. Measures to make services comprehensive, accessible, and better coordinated are structural to be sure, but they will miss their mark unless they are accompanied not only by adequate funding but also by a long list of other structural changes, including better education and training of those delivering the services and changes in public personnel policies that create sanctions against unproductive workers and rewards for those who are productive.

## The Search for the Panacea Solution

The third myth about the 1960s is that people believed there was a silver bullet, a single magic program that—if we could just find it—would solve all our ills. And in fact people have jumped from one quick fix and one panacea to another over the years. Even when an initiative was overly simplistic, we have not stayed with it long enough to see whether it would make a difference, and we have not taken the time to correct the flaws in the initial version to see whether it would work better when improved or redesigned.

The reactive myth of the 1980s—that nothing works, so why bother to try—is particularly understandable given the persistent naive faith that magic solutions exist and the massive unwillingness to stay with anything long enough to give it time to do any good.

There is a slightly more sophisticated version of these myths that deserves mention as well. This is represented by Senator Daniel Patrick Moynihan, who has said that the 1960s were "most successful . . . where we simply transferred income and services to a stable, settled group like the elderly. It had little success—if you like, it failed—where poverty stemmed from social behavior."

This is a vast oversimplification. If Senator Moynihan is saying that primary prevention is more successful than interventions with populations already manifesting social pathology, his observation is unremarkable, indeed obvious. But he seems also to be saying that there is no point in even trying to help those people whose need for services is so complex that it is difficult to ensure that the help will be effective. He seems to be questioning the value of crisis services and, for that matter, services of any kind to poor people who already have problems beyond their lack of income. He seems to write off vast groups of people: teenagers who get into trouble with the law or have babies, drug and alcohol abusers, many of the homeless, and others.

Our synthesis for the 1990s, Senator Moynihan notwithstanding, should be that, although there is no silver bullet, there are many interventions and many programs that do help, including many that demonstrably help multiproblem families. Nonetheless, while some families and some individuals within families can be helped by individual programs, broad progress depends on employing our endeavors in tandem. We have learned that the problems of many of the poor, and of high-poverty neighborhoods as a whole, are interrelated and difficult to separate. We cannot eliminate teenage pregnancy without dealing with education, health care, broader family issues, and employment opportunities. To promote individual self-sufficiency we need better schools, child care so parents can take jobs, and health coverage so people will not be tempted to stay on welfare in order to keep Medicaid. And again, to emphasize a key aspect of the point, many of the interventions that we know are effective are on behalf of people for whom "poverty stemmed from social behavior."

## WHAT HAVE WE LEARNED?

We know government has a role, but so do all of us. We know there are serious structural problems in the functioning of government and institutions that must be attended to. We know there are interventions that work but it must become possible to use them in combination and with sensitivity to specific locations. And we know we must act because we will be worse off if we do not.

In that context the question arises, how can we deliver more effective services? It is critically important to bear in mind that there are built-in severe barriers to change.

Legislative bodies at all levels of government take both budgeting and substantive action in relatively small increments. It is difficult to get the political decision-making system to act in comprehensive terms.

This situation is reinforced by the way interest groups relate to the political system. There are few multiservice interest groups. Most interest groups organize themselves according to their own field or discipline and have carved out counterpart power bases in legislative committees and executive agencies. Professionals want to maintain separate identities and power bases. They and their client groups lobby for their claim on scarce resources and do not want to share the limited pie.

Whether consciously or not, legislators and administrators alike act to maintain fragmentation as a way of dealing with scarce resources, because fragmentation rations use. If access points are unclear, fewer people will use the services and less money will be spent.

In fact, from a totally cynical point of view, fragmentation at the delivery end and block grants at the funding end are a perfect combination. Fragmentation reduces use, and block grants weaken constituency support for funding because no single constituency can be sure it will benefit from an increase in funding for the block. Recipient accountability is reduced by the use of block grants because there is no articulated set of standards against which to judge grantee performance. Congress does not easily see the successes that may have transpired at the local level with block grant money after it was handed out by the state (and it is hard for advocates and program administrators to amass the evidence), so it is more difficult to create momentum for increases in (or even to maintain) appropriations for the block.

## SEARCHING FOR MODELS

Buried in the inheritance from the past 30 years are a number of models of service and access that are worthy of mention as possible guides for effective services for children and families in the 1990s. Some of these efforts were stimulated by direct federal activity, others by indirect means; some came about because of state or local action; still others resulted from innovations within the voluntary sector. In some communities these efforts have been quite successful, while in other settings they have not produced desired effects. They are not large-scale, grand schemes; rather, they are modest efforts that are worthy of consideration for those concerned about future change.

These models focus on three different issues in the service process. Some of them intervene at the service delivery point, with multiservice and coordinated efforts at the point at which the client comes into the system. These efforts attempt to respond to clients' confusion when they confront a fragmented process and a bureaucratic maze that requires them to move from one service location to another. A second variety focuses on the planning and resource allocation process and seeks to intervene at the point at which budgets are made and top officials make determinations about service priorities. A third concerns place specificity: the design of services particularly aimed at defined geographic areas.

### Service Delivery and Access Models

### Multiservice Centers and Settlement Houses

There was never a federal program specifically designed to fund multiservice centers, but a number—the Roxbury Multi-Service Center in Boston is a typical example—were funded or stimulated by federal activity in the 1960s. The Door in New York City is an example of a multiservice center directed specifically at high-risk teenagers. The Beethoven Project in Chicago and the Casey Foundation initiatives are current examples directed at families in various ways. An older model, reformed and refurbished in the 1960s and 1970s in many cities, is the settlement house, which, properly led and administered, is a multiservice center by another name (or vice versa). A newer model, still more often a suggestion than a reality, is to colocate services in schools. The community schools movement and the Cities in Schools program, nongovernmental initiatives that began in the 1970s, have pursued this strategy with mixed results having more to do with the particular people involved in the individual cities than with the validity of the concept.

While every service a family might need cannot be located under one roof, these experiences indicate that it is possible to have a basic intake function as a core, and to have colocated on the premises such services as family counseling, legal services, primary health and mental health services, educational supplementation, child care, and recreational and community activities. Cities and counties could find it possible to locate an office to do eligibility for public assistance, food stamps, nutrition, and other relevant programs. All of this is far from simple, but it is possible.

This approach is different from the decentralization movement of the 1960s and 1970s. During that time there was a proliferation of neighborhood centers for separate programs: health centers, community mental health centers, and legal services offices. Each reflected a separate federal funding stream. In addition, there were separate state, county, and/or municipal social services offices and public health clinics and separate groups of job training and drug treatment programs, as well as nonprofit agencies offering a variety of specialized services, funded by combinations of United Way and public dollars and perhaps other local philanthropy.

In most cities, especially the large ones, it was difficult to rationalize these overlapping and uncoordinated centers. Each was naturally jealous of its own sovereignty, and most had vertical relationships with bureaucracies and funding sources that were in turn protective of their own sovereignty. While many of these centers are now defunct because of budget cuts, the underlying turf boundaries are problems that have not disappeared with the passage of time.

A related problem is that nongovernmental entities that seek to cut across categorical lines have an exceptionally difficult time getting the funds they need. Given that there is no multiservice center or settlement house "program," they must constantly hustle for public grants and contracts. At any one time they may have employment and training, drug treatment, teenage pregnancy prevention, Title XX, or any of a dozen other kinds of money. Often their current mix of activities is skewed by the kind of money that is available.

An especially pernicious problem is the timing of payment under grants and contracts. Typically, the city or county, whether under its own rules or federal or state rules, pays after the service is performed, so the private agency has to somehow front the money. Worse, payment is often unconscionably late. More than a few nongovernmental agencies have been driven out of business by this difficulty.

## Little City Halls

A few cities—New York and Boston come to mind—experimented with decentralized outposts of city government in the late 1960s and early 1970s.

Regardless of the name used, these public outposts—when and if competently staffed—could be revived as an access and referral point for services for children and families, cross-cutting the various public departments that offer services relevant to this clientele.

## Planning and Resource Allocation Models

### The Youth Bureau Model

If someone in the city or county mapped all of the services relevant to a particular clientele and sought, to the extent resources are available, to fill the gaps that show up, a better array of services should eventuate. If all of those in the area who were represented on the map had a copy of it when it was completed, better referral patterns should result.

In the field of youth services a number of states—New York is one—have adopted a system like the one described. Each county has a youth bureau that annually makes a youth services plan for the county. The state reviews the plan and occasionally rejects portions of it or asks for modifications. When the plan is approved the county is entitled to a certain amount of state funds to implement it, on a 50 percent matching basis. In New York State, at least, private providers are eligible for funding, and in some counties United Way supplies much of the local match. The funding is far from sufficient to cover all service needs for adolescents, but it is enough to cause every county to participate. The result is that services are typically more complete and referral patterns more clear than would otherwise be the case.

### Offices for Children

In the largest states it is difficult to contemplate the creation of an operating agency that would have under its jurisdiction all services for children and families if by that phrase one would mean to include public assistance, food stamps, social services, child welfare protective services, mental health, mental retardation, and juvenile justice. Smaller states have created such "super" agencies with mixed results, but in the biggest states such an agency would be extremely unwieldy (unless it was such a loose confederation as to be not a very meaningful consolidation).

What some states (and some local governments) have done, therefore, is to create an office for children as a part of the office of the chief executive. This office generally acquires the planning and legislative relations function for the relevant issues, at least with regard to major initiatives of the chief executive, and often has responsibility for the handling of particularly difficult individual cases of multiproblem (and therefore multiagency) children and families who might otherwise be shunted from agency to agency.

These offices cannot be a substitute for real services, however. In some cases, the efficacy of the offices for children has been overstated by elected officials seeking to claim they have done something for children when they either have insufficient resources to spend on needed programs or, even worse, have no wish to tackle problems directly on their merits.

## Place-Specific Models

A few of the past efforts were constructed on the concept of place specificity. This is especially relevant to areas in which there is a high concentration of poverty. Elsewhere, multidisciplinary access points and colocated services will improve accessibility and go some of the way toward improving quality. In areas of intense poverty, however, a sense of place in the design of services can play an even more fundamental role, as a part of a strategy to rebuild a feeling of neighborhood and community.

A key lesson to be drawn from the CAP, the Model Cities, and the multiservice center experiences is that, apart from a few individual multiservice centers and settlement houses, a fully funded, highly targeted, comprehensive approach in an area of great poverty has never really been tried.

One possible challenge to pursue for the 1990s would be a few such comprehensive approaches in areas of concentrated poverty. The desperate, multiproblem, multicrisis straits of such areas counsel a broad definition of comprehensiveness—one that goes beyond a single multiservice initiative, no matter how comprehensive that is in its work.

We should know by now that services alone will not cure poverty or rebuild a sense of community. A low-income family seeking help to find housing will not be helped by services if no housing is available at a price they can afford. Job training does not help when there are no jobs. Drug treatment is a drop in the ocean when there is a tidal wave of drugs in the street. Tutoring services will not make up for schools that do not teach. The problems of the street will engulf even the most sophisticated multiservice center if that initiative is taken in isolation.

For the 1990s a comprehensive approach in a single neighborhood of concentrated poverty must to the maximum possible extent go beyond services if it is to offer any hope of making a difference in the life of that area. Attention to housing, the schools, public safety and law enforcement, and economic development should be a part of a coordinated effort. This means that any such effort cannot be undertaken by the private sector by itself but must involve city government as well and state and federal funding for some portions of the endeavor.

A part of such a comprehensive approach in an area of intense poverty might be the rediscovery or reinvention of the settlement house in a contemporary form. This is a very complex task in itself. We cannot expect the model from the turn of the century to meet today's needs or surmount the built-in barriers to comprehensiveness in terms of government and politics and professional identities. A long list of problems must be addressed with the greatest of care.

Today, for example, intake workers in such a place would have to have a renaissance knowledge of human problems and the corresponding services to which one might make a referral. Professionals and other staff delivering services would have to be highly committed, able, and willing to accept the salaries ordinarily associated with such positions. And even a large investment in the settlement house itself would not create the myriad of necessary referral places or ensure their responsiveness to a telephone call seeking to make an appointment.

In order to minimize all of these problems, it is important that each service offered in such a center that is also a natural part of some larger agency and disciplinary world, whether it be health, mental health, or family services, be created with a relationship to the larger professional world of which it is a part. This is important for purposes of future funding, for coordination, and for the development of referral patterns.

The project should not be undertaken without a careful mapping of local perceptions of neighborhood and community needs for service and community participation in the design and policy direction of the services. Success in the 1990s requires a balancing of professional community involvement that eluded reformers in the 1960s.

Patience is a critical virtue, too. Each service may require a different license—the penetration in each case of yet another bureaucracy. Patience requires forbearance in the proclamation of success as well. The last thing we need is another round of prematurely raised expectations. No one should run off to advocate a government program to replicate the initiative until it has been in place long enough to prove its worth and has undergone rigorous evaluation.

## A PERSPECTIVE FOR THE 1990S

As this discussion has indicated, much has changed in the past 30 years. We have swung between strategies of extremes. We have moved from an environment of hope and possibility to one of limitations and despair. The fires of change of the 1960s have been dampened by the rains of fear, complexity, and cynicism. As the pendulum appears to be moving toward a new sense of activism and social responsibility, we must acknowledge that there are lessons to be learned from the experience of the past three decades. We offer five lessons for the future.

1. *Modesty and Humility.* We have learned that the social change we have attempted (and want to attempt in the future) is extremely difficult to

achieve. We are still far from knowing enough about what actually works and what does not, even though we know much more than we did in 1960 (and if we had the political will to fund fully the things that we know are successful, we would be far better off than we are now). While we want a society in which all citizens have hope for the future, we cannot raise expectations beyond some point of real possibility. Thus, even though we may seek to intervene in a few places in as massive a way as possible, we must at the same time do so cautiously, without grand promises and with the knowledge that we have embarked on a somewhat risky path. Panacea solutions of any kind are likely to fail.

2. *Limited Resources.* Few have to be reminded that programs for children and families are expensive, and it is extremely difficult to obtain funding for them in this era of budget limitation. While we know this, we sometimes have to be reminded that we have other resource limitations. Some of these limitations are of our own making and could be addressed. We do not have adequate expertise to guide our action. It has often been difficult to obtain support for program evaluation efforts and other data collection and monitoring schemes that provide program managers with information to use to modify ongoing programs. And we have found that time is also a scarce resource. Even small demonstration programs take much more time to put into operation than we usually give them. Frequently, the political system is not willing to wait for programs to develop before assessing their impact.

3. *Diversity.* Over the past 30 years we have learned a lot about the diversity of situations and populations around the country. We have been forced to acknowledge that the idiosyncracies of a state, locality, or even a neighborhood can determine the effectiveness of a particular program. We have recognized the importance of beginning programs or projects with a mapping of local perceptions of needs and finding ways to ensure a sense of participation and ownership by those who are the recipients of the services. At the same time, we have learned that change requires partnerships between many different actors: the professionals who actually deliver the services; the elected officials who must provide the resources for them, at least when they come to be replicated on a broad scale; the citizens who are the consumers of the services; and the administrators and managers at national, state, and local levels.

4. *Complexity.* Much of the negative perception about past programs stems from the unintended consequences that emerged from them. Seemingly simple strategies for change opened up numerous Pandora's boxes and created problems that seemed neverending. For example, a decision by a community to open up a multiservice center may confront an array of licensing and other bureaucratic requirements that effectively kills the effort. Similarly, schemes to address one set of problems may create other problems, particularly when eligibility requirements are affected.

5. *Synergy.* We know that the problems faced by children and families are interrelated and interdependent. While public safety, available jobs, school improvement, and affordable housing are separate problems, they are also closely related when we are talking about areas of concentrated poverty. Although for many families, even in such areas, there are single interventions that may have great impact, we have learned that others need multiple service interventions and still others need the benefit that comes from efforts to restore the basic institutions that make up a community. As we devise new schemes for the future, we are challenged to find ways to construct programs that have the ability to build on one another and operate in a related way.

We are well aware that these lessons pose a major dilemma. On one hand, the lessons of humility, complexity, and resource limitations counsel efforts at modest, incremental approaches to change. On the other, at least insofar as the problem of concentrated, intense, highly impacted poverty areas is concerned, it is time to seek a few demonstrations that are comprehensive on a synergistic scale never before attempted.

Although we know that there are no panacea solutions, we must find ways to create initiatives that demonstrate some level of visible effectiveness. These may be a few highly concentrated efforts in a small number of high-poverty neighborhoods, or new attempts to ease client access to services, or new endeavors to rationalize government funding streams and regulatory strictures, or new programs that respond to specific community based needs in areas in which single initiatives have promise of making a sufficient difference to be cost-effective. We can only hope that this is the beginning of a new public policy breakthrough that will bring us to a new era of public responsibility and compassion.

# State Financing Strategies That Promote More Effective Services for Children and Families

*Frank Farrow*
Center for the Study of Social Policy

As a growing number of states respond to the political, economic, and demographic pressures that are forcing change in children and family service systems, financing strategies are becoming an increasingly important part of their response. To some extent, this is simply because any effective service system must be adequately funded. Without sufficient dollars, no amount of improved service coordination or finely tuned response to families' needs will achieve the better outcomes for families and children that states seek. Beyond that, however, fiscal strategies are gaining attention because of recognition that methods of service finance directly affect the nature and outcomes of services. The ways in which funds are made available to state and local service systems help determine their priorities, shape the incentives that drive these systems, and ultimately influence how useful services are to families.

In the past few years, state administrators and legislators have become leaders in designing innovative financing mechanisms to reshape their service delivery systems. In conjunction with several foundation initiatives, such as those of the Edna McConnell Clark Foundation, the Annie E. Casey Foundation, and the Robert Wood Johnson Foundation, state officials are using financing changes as entry points from which to make even broader changes in state services.

This paper reviews several financing innovations that states are using to improve child and family services. It discusses the overall approach that underlies states' efforts; identifies specific fiscal strategies; and raises issues related to states' future development of financing strategies. The second paper in this volume by Drew Altman addresses financing strategies at the federal level.

## FINANCING AS A STRATEGIC ELEMENT
## IN IMPROVED STATE SERVICE SYSTEMS

States' use of new financing mechanisms takes many forms. However, there is a general strategic approach toward financing that underlies many states' efforts.

*This approach assumes that service financing should reflect and reinforce a new set of principles and characteristics for service delivery.* Consensus is emerging in many states about the directions in which child and family service systems must move if they are to be more effective. Public agencies are attempting to alter service systems to make them:

• Family-based, i.e., responsive to a child's needs in the context of his or her family and community;

• More comprehensive and flexible in meeting a child's and family's unique, specific needs;

• More likely to place decision-making authority at the community and neighborhood levels, rather than centralizing all decision making in state agencies;

• More balanced in terms of greater emphasis on developmental and preventive services that support families earlier and seek to avert crisis situations;

• More focused on outcomes; and

• Better able to ensure equity in services allocation.

Current financing methods undercut these directions, as is clear from numerous critiques of social service funding. The categorical nature of services financing still creates numerous specialized services in a community that defy workers' and families' best efforts to coordinate them. At the front line, families' needs usually have to be fit to available services, rather than the reverse. Since dollars are never sufficient for mandated services, allocations for developmental and preventive services remain even smaller in the context of overall service system expenditures.

States' new fiscal strategies attempt to restructure funding so that it supports the service delivery principles set forth above. If better outcomes are achieved when front-line workers adapt services to individual needs, then service funding should provide that flexibility. If decisions about which services to finance can be made more perceptively by local communities than by state agencies, then these decisions should be moved to the community level. If service priorities must be redirected toward earlier interventions, then financing mechanisms need to create incentives for front-end investments. Used in this way, financing becomes a way to reinforce new policy directions.

*States' new funding approaches also recognize that effective fiscal strategies must incorporate multiple funding sources and cut across tradition-*

*ally separate service domains.* Creating comprehensive service responses for children and families requires orchestration of a wide range of funding sources. States' perceptions of what constitutes an effective family service system is broadening to include social, health, education, mental health, juvenile justice, employment, housing, and other services. In the same way, states are working to coordinate (and in some cases consolidate) traditionally separate funding streams. Financing strategies are mixing funds across agency boundaries, using federal funds creatively in combination with state and local funds, and blending entitlement dollars with discretionary funds.

*Underlying most states' approaches is a third understanding: that financing strategies must make use of dollars already being expended in the service system.* Freeing dollars previously spent for one purpose and redirecting those same dollars for another purpose is a theme of several states' funding strategies. Such redirection usually involves shifts of funds from more restrictive to less restrictive forms of care. Thus, states are redirecting out-of-home placement dollars to in-home services, institutional support dollars to community-based care, and specialized treatment funds to more preventive care.

Not only does this emphasis on redirecting and redeploying funds reflect today's tight fiscal climate, but it also indicates a more general conclusion by state administrators: they can more plausibly justify increased appropriations when current dollars are spent most effectively.

*Finally, states' new funding approaches ensure that new financing strategies, by themselves, are unlikely to change service systems sufficiently. Fiscal changes require parallel alterations in service governance and service delivery technologies if they are to achieve states' goals for more effective service systems.* For example, as state agencies pool funds in order to achieve a common goal, they must also develop new, joint service definitions, new contracting procedures, and new interagency referral mechanisms. As states shift decision making concerning fund sources from a state agency to a local authority, they must determine how this change in governance power affects other aspects of the service delivery system.

Linking fiscal strategies to broader changes in service delivery is a positive step. It helps ensure that financing strategies are one part of a more fully developed service delivery system designed to achieve agreed-upon goals for children and families.

## PROMISING STATE STRATEGIES

States' funding innovations defy neat categorization. Many developed not as completely conceptualized new funding strategies, but as specific efforts to address a state's service delivery problems. These initiatives have usually been tempered both by political realities (some, for example, were altered substantially in the legislative process), and most are too recent for their impact to be addressed. The brief descriptions below emphasize the distinguishing characteristics of each state's approach and their potential to promote more coherent, responsive services to families.

*States' most basic approach to improved financing involves joint funding of services across agency lines in order to achieve common goals.* The purpose here is for agencies to share the costs of services that they would otherwise provide independently, thereby reinforcing a common policy direction and increasing the likelihood of more coordinated service delivery at the local level.

Tennessee's approach to funding family preservation services (crisis intervention services for families at imminent risk of having a child removed from the home) illustrates this approach.

In 1988, when Tennessee's legislative and executive branch leaders decided to develop family preservation services statewide, they sought to avoid adding further fragmentation to the state's service array. Unlike other states in which these services had grown separately in the child welfare, mental health, and juvenile justice agencies, Tennessee's agencies funded these programs jointly, with each of the serving agencies contributing a share of the cost.

With this pooled funding came other interagency agreements. In delivering these services, the three agencies agreed to accept a uniform program model for all of their families, decided on uniform contract specification for local programs, and are designing common training.

Cross-agency financing of this type is a small step, but for that reason can be a feasible step toward more flexible, less categorical financing. It has real benefits at the local level. The result of Tennessee's financing strategy, for example, will be that all family preservation services in a community will have uniform eligibility standards, regardless of whether a family receives this service due to problems of child abuse and neglect, delinquency or youth misbehavior, or a child's emotional problems. Local agencies contracting for this service will work toward common outcomes, use common referral procedures, and accept common standards to assess service quality. Most important, the state's achievement of uniform strategies for family preservation services is leading state officials to consider more extensive joint financing and cross-agency service delivery.

*A second strategy that goes further to restructure service financing involves allowing greater flexibility in the use of state-appropriated funds to meet family needs, with authority over those funds delegated to local entities.* This strategy represents a fundamental shift in financing arrangements—away from centralized, usually categorical state decision making, toward more flexible local control over funding decisions. Two states' different approaches illustrate the potential impact of this type of change.

Maryland recently enacted legislation that allows its Governor's Office for Children, Youth and Families (OCYF) to give local jurisdictions the authority to use funds appropriated for out-of-home care to provide in-home services for vulnerable children and families. The legislation applies to all types of out-of-home care, whether under the auspices of the child welfare, juvenile justice, mental health or education agencies.

As part of Maryland's broader reform initiative (aimed at helping the local communities to develop more comprehensive, family-based service systems, the OCYF is requiring localities to use these redirected out-of-home care funds in conjunction with other changes in local service planning and delivery. Local jurisdictions must develop an interagency plan for developing better services to families most at risk; must establish a new local entity that will have authority for spending the newly flexible dollars across agency lines; and must establish several core services, including family-based case management and family preservation services. While localities have latitude in the range of services they operate, they must agree to achieve outcomes established by the state. The incentive for localities to accept these conditions is that local communities retain 75 percent of any dollars saved by more efficient use of funds for reinvestment in their local service systems.

Maryland's initiative represents an attempt to redirect the state's large investment in out-of-home care to more cost-efficient and effective in-home and community services. As such, it potentially involves a large amount of state expenditures (over $200 million) but initially will affect a relatively narrow group of families, i.e., those at risk of out-of-home care.

A broader attempt to make funding more flexible and shift authority to the local level is represented by Iowa's decategorization initiative, which involves a wider array of children and family funding sources.

In 1987, the Iowa General Assembly passed legislation directing the state Department of Human Services to select two counties as demonstration sites for decategorizing child welfare services, with the intent of allowing the local jurisdictions to use these funds over a three-year period to develop a more client-centered as opposed to funding-stream-driven system.

A wide array of funding sources have been decategorized into a single fund for use by the two local jurisdictions, including funds in the mental health, juvenile justice, and child welfare systems, as well as such related services as day care and some services for the developmentally disabled. Education, Aid to Families With Dependent Children, and primary health care dollars were not included. The fund was intended to be revenue neutral, but allowance was made for yearly growth of the combined fund sources.

In each of the two pilot jurisdictions, an interagency group was established to plan the new constellation of services. A year into implementation of the new system, both jurisdictions have made changes in the allocation of funds compared with the allocations prior to decategorization. Home-based and community services have been expanded; out-of-home care has been held steady or reduced.

Most important, local jurisdictions have used the opportunity created by freeing up these dollars from past uses to rethink the values and directions underlying their service systems. Local officials feel they have charted a new course for family services, beginning to put in place a new continuum of care based on principles of supporting families in their homes and communities.

Iowa's decategorization of funds, like Maryland's redirection of out-of-home care dollars, is tied closely to other service system reforms. But in both cases, a significantly different financing strategy provided impetus for changes of a more wide-ranging nature than would otherwise have been possible.

*A third strategy being used by a growing number of states can be categorized as front-line service financing through use of flexible dollars.* This approach applies the concept of using funds to meet families' individual needs at the actual point of delivery. Workers are given access to funds in order to purchase on families' behalf the goods or services necessary to accomplish their goals.

This general approach has been implemented in different ways in different states. Alaska's Youth Initiative uses a version of this concept to pull together diverse and creative service packages on behalf of adolescents in the youth service system. Kentucky's "wraparound services" use the same concept to meet the needs of families experiencing difficulties in the care of their children, particularly emotionally disturbed children. Maryland's use of flexible dollars began in its Intensive Family Services program for a small number of highest-risk families, but it is now used throughout its protective services system. This "flex funds" concept is a centerpiece of family-based case management in Maryland's and North Dakota's Children and Family Services Reform Initiatives. In those states, generalist family service workers use these dollars to buy goods and services (rent deposits, emergency food, alcoholism treatment, emergency child care, etc.) as needed to stabilize families.

Judged by the dollars that flow through this mechanism in these states, this approach barely qualifies as a financing strategy. Dollar amounts available per family range from a low of several hundred dollars to a high of several thousand. But judged by the capacity to ensure immediate response to families—in ways that mean the most to families—this method of channeling funds, and thus financing services, warrants wider exploration.

The strategies discussed to this point represent attempts to overcome the worst effects of categorical funding. *A fourth group of state financing strategies involves using federal entitlement programs to expand the fund-*

*ing base available for child and family services.* This strategy differs from the others described here. It is less concerned with restructuring funding to local communities and to families and instead aims at ensuring that all available funds are used to expand services. By using federal funds fully, states and localities can then use other dollars to pay for service costs that are not reimbursable through federal sources.

Expanding states' service financing through entitlements can be done in two ways. First, states use entitlements to cover as broad a range of services as federal law will allow and as state budgets can accommodate. Many states are beginning to examine the new Medicaid provisions of the past several years to determine how to use them to underwrite services. Medicaid's targeted case management provisions are already being used to expand state services to children with emotional disturbances and developmental disabilities. Similarly, Medicaid's expanded Early and Periodic Screening, Diagnosis, and Treatment (EPSDT) provisions are being scrutinized (and in some states are already in use) for their potential to reimburse a wider range of service costs as part of the treatment plan for an eligible child.

In deciding how to use Medicaid financing, states must weigh such factors as whether the danger of overmedicalizing services is offset by fiscal advantages, whether the per child reimbursement of Medicaid funding undercuts family-based service planning, etc. As with other entitlement funds, Medicaid's funding potential must be examined in the context of the service delivery structure that a state is trying to establish.

The second way in which states are using entitlement funding to improve service systems is by claiming entitlements more aggressively for costs previously paid by state and local funds, thereby freeing those state and local funds for reinvestment in service systems improvements. In the past few years, Title IV-E of the Social Security Act has been used in this way. By expanding Title IV-E claims to the maximum extent allowed under federal law, states can achieve a sudden and dramatic revenue increase. State funds freed by this infusion of federal funds can then be used to make more rapid and substantial changes to child and family services than might otherwise be possible.

States' individual financial gains from Title IV-E in the past year have ranged from several million dollars to more than $30-40 million, depending on the size of the state. While not all of these funds have been reinvested in family services, a significant amount was. Most important, in keeping with a strategic approach to service financing, a significant number of states are using these increased Title IV-E claims to build more effective service systems.

The financing strategies outlined here are just some of the states' new approaches. Other approaches are developing rapidly, raising questions about future directions of funding innovations.

## ISSUES FOR THE FUTURE

Several trends seem likely to influence states' financing strategies for child and family services over the next decade.

The first is discernible from today's innovations. Many states are attempting to put in place financing structures that are genuinely child- and family-centered, that is, newly responsive to individual child and family needs and community priorities. The basic elements of such a system might involve: (1) front-line flexible funding that gives workers discretion over dollar expenditures; (2) noncategorical allocations to local communities, with state-established expectations and outcomes but allowing local decisions about service priorities; and (3) incremental decategorization of existing funds into these more flexible funding structures. (The states participating in the Annie E. Casey Foundation's reform initiative are building such systems, as are other states, but none is fully developed.) Many issues must be addressed as such systems grow:

• To what extent can and should current funding be consolidated as part of flexible funding arrangements, either at the community or the client level?

• How should flexible fund allocations be combined with predetermined funding levels for core, mandated services?

• Can alternative accountability structures be put in place (outcome expectations and measures, etc.) to replace the minimal accountability now obtained through prescriptive, categorical funding?

• Politically, can effective advocacy be marshaled on behalf of flexible funding?

The second issue for states seeking improved service financing is how funding can be provided through a more stable, entitlement-oriented mechanism. Part of the pressure for broader use of Medicaid financing for children and family services comes from states' desire to shift away from social service funding sources to an ensured entitlement financing base.

A similarly motivated (at least in part) state interest is developing to link family services to schools and to education funding. Better ties between educational services and child and family services make sense programmatically, but they also raise intriguing financing possibilities. Key questions here are:

• Can child and family services be more closely associated with the health care and educational systems without taking on the more negative aspects of the medical and educational models?

• Can states find ways to combine their greater use of entitlements with the innovative, highly flexible family service funding described above?

Fueled by simultaneous pressures to control costs and improve services, states are likely to continue their financing innovations. The challenge will be to direct these new approaches in a way that, in fact as well as in theory, makes financing structures more rather than less useful to families, and more rather than less likely to promote effective outcomes.

# The Challenges of Services Integration for Children and Families

*Drew Altman*
Henry J. Kaiser Family Foundation

This paper covers two topics: strategies for financing integrated services for children and families, as well as some of the down sides of services integration as a strategy at all. These two topics may not be as contradictory as they appear at first blush, since the considerable difficulties of untying the Gordian knot of financing is one of the reasons why integration may not be the best, or certainly the only, strategy for all of us in the field to pursue.

## FINANCING SERVICES INTEGRATION

Reforming the financing of services for children and families is a means to an end. We should do so to the extent that it is necessary to enhance the effectiveness of the services we provide. The argument that is made—and I have made it myself—is that the categorical nature of programs make it difficult to tailor services to real needs. All that is true, but it is important not to exaggerate the significance of the financing issue. Without any change in financing, schools could be mandated to make their facilities available to the community. Welfare case workers could be moved out of their offices and into community settings. Community agencies could agree on uniform assessment tools and abide by service plans. Schools and Head Start agencies could work together more closely. All of these things and many more could be accomplished without major changes in the way in which we finance the services we provide.

After many years as an advocate of financing reform, I have become convinced that the obstacles to services integration are as much professional, organizational, and political as they are a function of the absence of this or that federal waiver, pooled financing scheme, or other new financing arrangement. Without question, reforming financing will strengthen our efforts, but it is not a magic cure.

Moreover, if our service system is poorly arranged, it is also underfunded. Welfare checks provide support at a fraction of the federal poverty level. Staff salaries in community agencies yield turnover rates of 40 percent or more. And 15 percent of the population in the average state lacks health insurance coverage. It hardly needs saying that you can't pool, capitate, insure, or guarantee funding with nothing. When I took over as human services commissioner in New Jersey in 1986, we were paying physicians $7.00 under Medicaid for a general office visit. No matter how you slice it, $7.00 will not go very far. Reforming the financing of services for children and families will not solve the underfunding problem.

That said, there is little question but that more flexible funding arrangements and more permanent funding streams would help in our efforts to make services for children and families more effective. What follows then are two modest suggestions to move us forward on the financing front at the national level. The paper by Frank Farrow in this volume focuses on state-level initiatives.

## A Vehicle for Federal Action

There sits in the White House a now virtually inactive entity known as the Low-Income Opportunity Advisory Board (LIOAB). Established through executive order by President Reagan, the LIOAB brings together in the White House all the federal agencies responsible for the major social programs. It has high-level representation and is directed by senior White House staff. The LIOAB has the authority not just to tinker with categorical programs, but to help effect the thoroughgoing changes necessary to enable states and communities to pool financing, to reorganize services, and generally to change the rules and try out new approaches. (Technically, the board's authority does not supersede the authority of individual agencies or agency heads, but its recommendations amount to the same thing.)

Can the board help? There is precedent that says it can. Quietly, near the end of the Reagan administration, the board provided federal waivers for no less than 16 major state and local welfare and social services experiments. These projects tested major changes in how the welfare system worked and together helped lay the groundwork for nation legislation. Not all were state-level initiatives; a variety of community-based efforts were undertaken as well.

The LIOAB could be revitalized tomorrow and asked to play the same role for services for children and families. Using the board, the President could establish a national integrated children's services initiative, soliciting proposals from state and local government and communities, with a commitment to establish 10 to 20 major efforts. These projects would have at their heart a single point of contact for children and families in a defined geographic area and pooled financing, bringing together multiple funding streams and giving professionals the flexibility to design individual family service plans.

By way of example only, let's imagine that through this approach we created a new entity called Family Maintenance Organization (FMO). The FMO would allocate resources from a fixed amount for each enrolled child or family, established by pooling existing funds. Professionals would have the flexibility to devote resources to preventive services before major problems occur, such as home visiting for families in crisis whose children are at high risk of foster care placement. All services would be neighborhood based.

This is just an example; capitation need not be the approach taken. Funds could also be pooled at the statewide, regional, organizational, family, or individual level. The important point is that flexibility is provided to meet service needs and that bills for services provided are paid. In an initiative such as this the exact approaches taken would have to bubble up from the local or state level. No one knows what approach is best, and circumstances vary greatly across the country.

To get started, the President could announce the new initiative. The LIOAB would establish guidelines and solicit proposals, implementing 10 to 20 integrated service programs for children. If the White House was not interested, the Department of Health and Human Services could take the lead itself. Secretary Louis Sullivan has a keen interest in this approach and jurisdiction over a majority of the relevant programs. But to really bring in programs administered by the departments of Labor, Agriculture, and Education and to avoid conflict with the Office of Management and Budget, it would be better if the White House took the lead.

In the alternative, Congress could mandate that the board take on this job. But it would be better if the board/administration were to seize the initiative itself. Congressional mandates aside, bureaucracies work best when they actually want to carry out the assignments with which they have been charged.

In theory, such an initiative could be undertaken on a revenue-neutral basis, but I see no reason why we should assume this going in. Figuring out whether a new approach costs or saves money used to be considered a legitimate undertaking in the federal government. The idea that demonstrations should only be undertaken (and waivers granted) when they are guaranteed to save money is one of recent vintage, and the depth of feeling on this issue in the Bush administration has yet to be tested.

## Financing School-Based Services

Perhaps the leading example of services integration for children and families in the country right now is the school-based services movement. I believe that school-based services hold great promise for the future. For reasons well known to this audience, it is absolutely essential to break down the barriers that exist between the schools and our health and human services systems. Yet, with some exceptions, school-based services programs are inadequately funded and rely, to their peril, on "soft" money from foundations and government. This is a promising strategy that needs a better funding base if it is to be institutionalized and taken to scale.

One step that could make a big difference would be to make school-based services programs participating Medicaid providers. My guess is that between 70 and 95 percent of the young people using school-based health and human services programs are Medicaid-eligible. Moreover, in most states the majority of services provided are covered by Medicaid and EPSDT. Thus, opening up the Medicaid-funding spigot could very significantly help to stabilize school-based projects. With about 50 percent of Medicaid-eligible children not now receiving services, it could also go a long way toward reaching the underserved.

To my knowledge this could be done immediately. Without any change in state or federal law or a federal waiver, states could define the characteristics of school-based services programs eligible to participate in their Medicaid programs and reimburse for services covered in their state Medicaid plans. Alternatively, the federal government could mandate that states offer participation in Medicaid to school-based services programs meeting specified standards laid out in federal rules. Participation in Medicaid could also be used as a carrot to leverage more comprehensive services than Medicaid can cover, by stipulating that eligibility to participate would depend on the ability to provide a range of services beyond those actually covered by the state's Medicaid program. In this way, Medicaid could be used to encourage the colocation and coordination of a broader range of services that children and families need.

## THE PITFALLS OF INTEGRATED SERVICES

Having said that integration and coordination can improve services for children and families, and that changes in financing can assist in the implementation of services integration schemes, I also offer the caution that we keep services integration in perspective as we consider the full range of options available in assisting children and families in need. Our goal is effective services, and services integration is but one approach. Indeed, it runs the risk of becoming today's fad, inheriting that mantle from case management—that often so ill-defined buzzword of the last 10 years.

First, the most practical problem with services integration is that it is so hard to do. We are much better at mailing checks and expanding existing programs than we are at the slow process of institutional, professional, and bureaucratic change. Increasing the earned income tax credit, increasing welfare grants, expanding Medicaid eligibility, paying for more child care, guaranteeing minimum child support payments . . . if we can find the dollars, we know that these are things we can do well. As this institutional reformer of long standing knows from firsthand experience, one of the benefits of income versus services strategies is their "doability" in the real world. The best strategy (services integration) is not always the best policy choice in practice.

Second, as we always discuss, services integration programs are inherently difficult to take to scale. Comprehensive, intensive, preventive, neighborhood-based, family-centered strategies are expensive and are usually highly leadership dependent. Such approaches will do a lot for a limited number of families and children. Broader changes in big public systems (such as welfare, Medicaid, the tax structure, or the child welfare system) may do less on an individual basis (and if poorly crafted may do nothing at all) but can reach many more families in need. This trade-off between breadth and depth of impact is an important one to keep in mind as we debate the merits of this or that interesting local services integration scheme.

Third, expertise and specialization can make a difference, although they are in disrepute these days. I sometimes think that case management and primary care are solutions we prescribe at least a little more often for poor people than we do for ourselves.

Fourth, as noted earlier, services integration can do little to add dollars to an underfunded system. Nor is it likely to save as much money as is often alleged. Too often it will supplement rather than replace existing services and identify further unmet needs that will cost money in the end.

Fifth, as political scientists have longed observed, categorical programs win greater funding and are more resistant to the budget ax when it threatens to fall. This is no small consideration in this period of federal deficits and hard-hit state budgets.

Sixth (and to take on everything we hold dear), primary prevention— usually one of the key underpinnings of services integration schemes—is right-minded but also somewhat inefficient from a policy point of view. The reason for this is that in primary prevention resources are devoted shotgun style to a large number of individuals and families who might never develop problems at all, and on whom public resources might not have ever been spent. This is a problem that is best solved by targeting primary prevention activities on the highest-risk groups, but our success in targeting in this way has been less than perfect over the years. Secondary prevention, by contrast, deals with known individuals with known problems, on whom considerable sums would surely be spent. Once again, the best intervention is not necessarily the best policy choice.

Seventh, I worry that in our recent emphasis on intensive, integrated services, we confuse the best strategy for a minority group or the poor with the best strategy for all. Certainly, for multiproblem children and families, and for children in contact with the protective services system, the most comprehensive service interventions make sense. But in our rush to make everything comprehensive, we should not forget that most poor Americans do not neatly fall into these categories. Most are working and move in and out of poverty, or on and off of welfare, rather than remaining for long spells. For these low-income Americans, targeted interventions—some needed job or skills training, health coverage during a transition to work, assistance with child care costs, etc.—can make a huge difference. No doubt comprehensive, case-management-driven service systems would benefit almost all Americans, but they are probably not the best policy choice for assisting the largest number of America's poor.

Eighth, and most broadly, most calls for integrated services would place those service efforts in the context of broader community mobilization schemes. While the grass roots nature of these community-based strategies have brought liberals and conservatives together in support of integrated services as an approach, I worry about community-based strategies as our main weapon in the fight against poverty in the decade ahead. The results of such efforts— bubbling up, community by community across the country—are certain to be quite variable and difficult to sustain. Changes in big programs, systems, and institutions, by contrast, are likely to be more universal in nature and, arguably, more lasting in their effects.

So, thinking about the role and difficulties of financing services integration has led me to want to keep the strategy itself in perspective. All responsible advocates of services integration make exactly these points. Nevertheless, I do sometimes feel that those of us in the business of helping children and families are in danger of letting this particular strategy dominate our thinking these days. Our goal is to help children and families, and there are a variety of routes to that end.

# The Role of Training and Technical Assistance in The Promotion of More Effective Services for Children

*Douglas W. Nelson*
Annie E. Casey Foundation

Over the past decade, critical reflection on the state of human services has given rise to a growing consensus on both what's wrong with the way services are provided to at-risk families and children and the essential elements of a system of practice that presumably would work much better. It has, for example, become common among reform-minded analysts to use the descriptions "fragmented," "reactive," "categorical," "inaccessible," "arbitrary," and "unrelated to actual needs" as a means of explaining the failure of existing helping systems to have their hoped-for impact on outcomes for at-risk children and their parents. At the same time, confidence has grown dramatically in the ability of "preventive," "flexible," "family-centered," "collaborative," "intensive," and "individualized" services to make a real difference in the lives and prospects of those who benefit from them.

This widening agreement has emerged from two primary streams of analysis: first, logical critique of the mismatch between the typical characteristics of families in need and the characteristics of mainstream service system responses and, second, an empirical assessment of the attributes common to various programs and services that appear to work. Taken together, these two modes of evaluation have fostered a fairly distinct image of where children and family services ought to be going. The challenge that remains (and increasingly preoccupies the advocates of change) is the strategic challenge of how to get there.

Obviously central to this challenge is the issue of training. If routine provider-client interactions are really to become more voluntary, discretionary, collaborative, and family-centered, then future front-line workers will need both basic academic and in-service training that enables mastery of the core skills implicit in this "new" practice.

In practical terms, this need implies substantial change for both social work education and the kind of in-service training made available to public- and voluntary-sector workers. In each setting, much greater emphasis will have to be accorded to the family context in assessing and addressing problem issues; to communication and relational skills that encourage mutuality, trust, and equality between provider and client; and to the diagnostic and resources knowledge that can enable workers to assume broader individual responsibility for identifying and addressing the diverse and changing range of issues that actual families experience. These subject areas will need to become more central—not only in the curricula of social work schools and in formal orientations of new workers, but also in the ongoing supervisory and evaluation systems that serve as a de facto form of continuing training to front-line professionals.

Even more crucial, perhaps, may be the need to create a decentralized and program-based network of training resources to support the dissemination of reformed practice skills. The whole thrust of the new practice perspective is to diminish a priori, standardized, authority-driven, input-focused interventions in favor of ad hoc, situational, collaborative, and outcome-oriented interactions with clients. The skills implied by these new practice characteristics almost by definition resist reduction to the generalizability appropriate to textbooks or to the codification typical of practice manuals. Instead, they lend themselves far more readily to being taught through case illustrations, through observation of actual practice by experienced workers, and through constructive criticism of student work in actual service settings.

Given all this, I think a fairly strong case can be made for envisioning exemplary service settings and programs as the critical institutional foundations upon which we should plan and build a capacity to educate and train a newly oriented cadre of front-line child and family workers. In concrete terms, this would mean a commitment to identify and fund (within states and communities) specific programs or agencies to serve as learning centers for the training or retraining of professionals. At least some of the workers in such designated lab programs would be supported to serve as faculty to less experienced observer-students, interns, or residents preparing to take service jobs in other agencies and programs. Faculty from learning center programs could also travel to provide periodic in-service training to workers in their own program settings through case consultation, evaluative observation, or more formal training events.

The suggestion is hardly novel. Indeed, the role that Homebuilders program staff have played in orienting line workers in new family preservation programs around the country serves as a visible example of the model. The point here, however, is that the model needs to be more consciously and planfully developed and embraced as a core strategic component of all local and state efforts to expand genuinely family-centered responses to the needs of children. Furthermore, the model ought not be conceived simply as a marginal supplement to academic training or as a stopgap remedy to the deficiencies in current social work curricula. Rather, program-based training ought to be recognized as a primary and durable vehicle for conveying the values, knowledge, and skills essential to a new kind of service provision.

Regardless of the merits of the specific notions advanced above, there can be little debate about the fundamental importance of worker training. Ultimately, the quality of any family service reform will be conditioned by the skills and values of those who provide help to children and their parents. Having granted this, however, there is also a strong need to put the issue of provider training in context. It is important to emphasize that, although inadequate worker training may contribute to fragmented, discontinuous, coercive, and partial service delivery systems, it did not cause these system defects; it does not explain them; nor would providing the best practice training possible remedy them.

The fact is that the nature of most current worker-client interactions is a product, not of worker values or skills, but rather the fiscal, statutory, political, informational, and organizational environments in which child and family service systems operate and evolve. It is the categorical nature of funding streams and bureaucratic organization that really dictates that most interactions with multiproblem families will be partial, uncoordinated, or inaccessibly complex. It is the input-based information systems, process-based accountability systems, and divergent eligibility requirements that virtually guarantee that the best-intended efforts to serve families will simply not be flexible enough, family-centered enough, intense enough, timely enough, or tailored enough to achieve their intended objectives. In sum, it is probably fair to conclude, as Lisbeth Schorr has written, "that all the major attributes of effective services are fundamentally at odds with the dominant ways that most large institutions and systems are funded and the way they . . . ensure accountability, quality, and equity."

This straightforward assessment actually points up the most critical training and technical assistance challenge confronting the effort to expand and institutionalize effective services for children. Put simply, it is the need for a level of fiscal, organizational, political, and management expertise sufficient to enable proponents of more effective services to create institutional and policy environments in which those very services can survive and expand. The regrettable reality is that most state and local managers of child and family services have precious little of this kind of expertise. On the whole, they lack familiarity with the origin, interplay, and intricacies of the funding streams that powerfully influence the amount and kind of services available. By and large, they are unprepared to design and develop outcome measures and accountability systems that would foster more tailored goal setting and greater worker discretion at the point of delivery. Finally, it must also be observed that most current child services policy makers are relatively untrained in the arts of public education and political organization—arts that are critical to creating a more appropriate set of public expectations for services to at-risk children.

The question that all this obviously raises is how do we bring these crucial skills, abilities, and interests more fully into the movement for better services to children and families. A short-run answer probably lies in increasing the cadre of national consultants who are able to provide fiscal, organizational, legal, and automation (management information systems) assistance in support of state and local efforts to expand service initiatives that work. The Clark Foundation-supported technical assistance forum illustrates one attempt to cultivate and coordinate this kind of capacity on a national level. A strong case, however, can be made that a far larger and more generalized national technical capacity is already urgently needed.

In the long run, though, the paramount goal has to be creating greater fiscal, organizational, and political management capacity at the state and the community levels. Real knowledge and experience in how to impact the larger environments in which services are delivered has to become a more prominent part of the skills repertoire of child advocates, child service administrators, and even front-line practitioners.

Given this, it probably makes sense to specify building local capacity as a more explicit objective of any existing or future national technical assistance strategy in these areas. Perhaps even more important, some consideration ought to be given to revising the conventional conceptions of the qualifications and credentials that are most relevant in the recruitment of administrative and policy-level staff within child serving organizations. In some instances, experience in the manipulation of state-local funding ratios may contribute to building intensive, community-based services to youth far more than the most thorough knowledge of the stages of adolescent development.

In the end, this whole argument has implications for basic education and training in social work and social policy. At the very least, it suggests that we need to be more aggressive in emphasizing how economic, political, and organizational contexts powerfully determine the social work that is actually practiced and the social policy that is actually implemented. That knowledge, by itself, would go a long way to more fully empowering future professionals to more fully empower the families they will serve.

# Collaboration as a Means, Not an End: Serving Disadvantaged Families and Children

*Olivia Golden*
Kennedy School of Government
Harvard University

The purpose of this paper is to offer a framework for thinking about collaboration as a strategy for successful service delivery to children and families, particularly the most needy children and families. The paper aims to stimulate discussion by raising some central questions and offering a single perspective on how to resolve them; it does not aim to provide a comprehensive account of what we know or how we ought to proceed.

Discussions of collaboration often begin from an account of successful collaborations and the lessons they teach us. However, to start there begs three important questions:

(1) Why is collaboration a good thing? That is, why should we be interested in it in the first place?

(2) What is collaboration? What are the important types of collaboration for us to pay attention to?

(3) Why is collaboration so hard? That is, what did these programs have to overcome to become successful?

This paper starts with these questions, because my own experience of studying successful programs convinces me that we cannot do justice to the lessons from program experience if we ignore them, if we implicitly assume that collaboration in itself is a good and sufficient purpose, or that the barriers to collaboration are obvious. Furthermore, whether or not we have to answer these questions in order to *understand* program experience, we certainly have to answer them in order to persuade public officials to *act* on program experience, since those officials are unlikely to be interested in collaboration for collaboration's sake—and they are likely to be concerned about the likely obstacles.

Having offered answers to these initial questions, the paper then goes on to suggest promising future directions. It tries to explain how successful collaborations have overcome the barriers to collaboration, providing a tentative list of elements these successes share. It concludes by proposing four opportunities for change, selected in the hope that the forum's recommendations could make a difference.

## WHY IS COLLABORATION A GOOD THING?

For some writers on collaboration, its value is self-evident. The present system is fragmented, meaning that service deliverers and the agencies they work in do not know about each other's services, talk to each other, work together, or even share a common language or perception of the problem. Therefore, the solution is collaboration: service deliverers and program administrators ought to bridge these gaps.

As Bruner (1990b) and Altman (in this volume), among others, have recently noted,[1] this is not a very satisfying account of the reasons for collaboration, for several reasons. First, it is not obvious that collaboration always has good rather than bad effects on services for families and children. Collaboration might lead agencies to carry out their differentiated, precollaboration mission less well: for example, an eligibility worker asked to assess families' service needs and refer them to family support programs might get benefit checks out less quickly or take information gained from the assessment inappropriately into account in the benefit determination. Collaboration might lead a program that has been effective on Schorr's criteria to become less so, if it collaborates with a more rigid, bureaucratic program and its mission and culture are diluted. For example, staff in a teenage parent program I visited for recent research on welfare and children's services were very nervous about the emphasis on rules that their (ultimately unsuccessful) collaboration with a local welfare agency was, they thought, imposing on their services. And for some families, there seems to be nothing wrong with the present system of services and therefore little to be gained from collaboration: many middle-class families, for example, may be able to ensure that a child gets to school and gets to the doctor without seeing any particular reason why the school system and the health system ought to communicate (Bruner, 1990b:8). Second, collaboration has costs for staff. It requires time, often a great deal of time, for staff to learn about each other's purposes and activities, develop a common language, work on practical problems, and resolve conflicts (Bruner, 1990b:33). Collaboration may also be costly when it shifts the kind of skills workers

---

[1]For an argument that goes even further to make the case that collaboration is not a desirable route for human services, see Weiss (1981).

need—for example, by adding negotiation and problem-solving skills to narrower technical skills—and therefore requires retraining and perhaps re-deployment or attrition of staff. And collaboration can be costly in terms of increased levels of staff tension, at least in the short run: questions that once could be decided simply by one or two people now require an ex-tended process, and jobs that once were private turf are invaded by outsid-ers (see for example Morrill and Gerry, no date; Bruner, 1990b:7).

Thus, we need a better justification for collaboration as a solution than simply that services are fragmented. In particular, to advocate for collabo-ration in services to the most needy families and children, we need to believe that collaboration will typically lead to better service delivery. Why should this be?

The answer, it seems to me, lies in the findings of Schorr and others about the characteristics of disadvantaged families and the way those char-acteristics interact with the system that serves them (for a longer discussion, see Golden, 1990). For families and children who have multiple needs— needs that are related to each other in complex causal chains—and who lack knowledge, self-confidence, money, and skill in handling bureaucracies, the fragmented service system imposes enormous burdens. And these burdens may well fall most heavily on those least able to cope: the most fragile, those with the most complex needs, those with the fewest resources. For example, a case manager in a program for low-income teenage parents re-ported on the difficulties that the teenagers' lack of education posed for their dealings with the health system, in the case (which she reported was not rare) of teenage parents of babies with chronic illness (Golden, 1990:48):

> The one I have now without a bladder—this baby will have multiple surgery, and the mother has been tested at third grade and she doesn't understand what is going on. So I have to go along to interpret what the nurses are saying.

For these families, fragmentation is indeed destructive, because it means that no matter which fragment of the system they enter, which door they go through, they will find someone who can respond only to a tiny piece of their problem. Without the capacity to work the system themselves, they will end up lost unless the system itself provides the glue to keep the pieces together. Therefore, service deliverers who are to succeed with these fami-lies must identify and respond to needs that cross system boundaries, or in Lisbeth Schorr's terms, "adapt or circumvent traditional professional and bureaucratic limitations when necessary to meet the needs of those they serve" (Schorr, 1988:258). Unless these service deliverers are able to do everything from educate a young child to care for a sick baby to counsel a suicidal mother within their own organizations, this demand requires that they collaborate.

Charles Bruner (1990b) takes this analysis one step further, sorting out three different types of families whose needs particularly require collaboration. First is the family with many needs at a crisis or near-crisis stage and many human services providers already involved. For this family, the key benefit of collaboration is that the providers will talk to each other, stop conveying to the family contradictory or at least unrelated expectations, and think about the impact of their interactions with different family members on the family as a whole. An example from my own research, offered by case managers in Oklahoma's Integrated Services System, illustrates the nature and benefits of collaboration in such a case (Golden, 1990:49-50):

> A seven-year-old boy came to the attention of a school principal because of both physical and emotional health problems. The boy had long been prone to seizures and self-destructive behavior and was just starting to threaten other children. When the principal called IFS [Integrated Family Services], he found that IFS was already working with the family because the mother was on AFDC and herself had multiple problems. The IFS worker called a meeting of all the agencies who had contact with the family to talk about the child's needs. As a result, the boy was admitted and sent to a diagnostic center for several months of testing and treatment; the mother received needed services such as mental health treatment and literacy training; and the Child Protective Services worker changed her mind about the possible outcomes for the case and concluded that the mother had the potential to be an adequate parent.

Second is the family with many low-level needs that add up to serious risk for the child. Such a family may have limited contact with three or four service systems—the public schools, the unemployment office, the city hospital, and perhaps the welfare department—but it probably won't meet anyone's criteria for intensive services. Yet a collaborative approach might well identify it as a family for whom there are real opportunities for intervention that could change a child's life. Bruner (1990b:10) illustrates this point with an example:

> Johnny, a seven-year-old first grader, is behind his fellow students in reading and other activities. He often is late to school, as his mother works nights and sometimes does not get up in time to get him off to school. There are no books in Johnny's home, and his mother, a dropout from ninth grade, views the school system with a sense of powerlessness and distrust. Johnny and his mother live together in a ten-year-old trailer, and Johnny frequently gets colds from the drafts through the trailer.

Third, Bruner notes the role of collaboration in serving families whose problems are related to community- or neighborhood-wide concerns: unsafe housing, poverty, violence on the streets, limited access to health care

(p. 10). In this kind of example, collaboration is important because of the interlocking problems in the neighborhood and because failures by a wide range of public service systems have contributed to those problems, not necessarily because of the interlocking problems of the family itself. Thus, the purpose of this kind of collaboration is to produce changes in various service policies and in the allocation of resources, not necessarily changes in the ways individual families are treated.

Collaboration, then, is not an end in itself but a means to better services for families and children. I have argued that it is nonetheless a crucial means for many of the most needy families: those who cannot themselves integrate a fragmented system to get what they need, because of the complexity of their needs, their financial and other difficulties in access, their isolation or lack of self-confidence. And collaboration may also be a crucial part of the solution for families not themselves fragile or isolated who live in neighborhoods characterized by the failure of a whole interlocking set of public systems.

## WHAT IS COLLABORATION?

In the account above of why we should care about collaboration, I have offered examples of collaboration but not a definition. One important reason for that choice is that the purpose we have in mind for collaboration, meeting the needs of fragile families and children, is difficult enough without artificially limiting the possible techniques by defining them away. For example, there is no way to know a priori whether collaboration at the street-level, where services to families are delivered, has more or less potential to change their lives than collaboration at the state level, which affects the decisions of top policy staff. Therefore, I propose that we define collaboration as simply as possible and concentrate not on its boundaries but on the multiple ways of carrying it out.

A simple definition might be that collaboration involves separate organizations working together. The key point here is that collaboration is not the same as merger: a collaborative effort retains different organizations with their separate specialties and points of view. Therefore, for a collaboration to succeed, each organization must see a contribution from the collaboration to its own mission and purposes. A collaboration between a school and a health clinic, for example, does not imply that they can now substitute for each other, but rather that they are working together in a way that each (if it is a successful, ongoing collaboration) sees as helping it do its own job better. Not surprisingly, this feature of collaboration has implications both for barriers to collaboration and for the approaches taken by successful collaborators.

An enormous variety of activities could fit under this simple definition. Classifying these activities into types has two purposes: to enable us to scan what is already going on or contemplated, and to help us think up new activities that seem promising. Three dimensions of collaborative activities seem to me useful in such a classification: *mission*, defined either as a vision to be achieved or a problem to be solved; *level*, such as service delivery, city, and state; and function, such as outreach and intake, evaluation, development of new resources, and policy design. Thus, a collaboration might have the mission of reducing teenage pregnancy, be organized at the city level, and focus on achieving its mission through several functions: joint outreach by service deliverers who see out-of-school teenagers (public health nurses, community youth workers), direct service delivery in the schools (life planning programs), improved and more personalized brokering of services (a nurse who will personally follow up on a young woman's referral to a local health clinic for a family planning appointment), and cross-training of service deliverers. Another collaboration might have the mission of serving children with multiple disabilities who fall through gaps in service, might be organized at the state level, and might plan to achieve the mission primarily through functions like the exchange of information on caseload and service characteristics, evaluation of services (for example, the identification of gaps), and the development of priorities for new programs and resources.

Table 1 offers examples of collaborative activities now being carried out or proposed at each level, to suggest the broad range of possibilities. As the next section suggests, we will need to consider all the flexibility and all the opportunities this broad range offers if we are to overcome the many and fundamental obstacles.

## WHY IS COLLABORATION SO HARD?

To the doctor, the child is a typhoid patient; to the playground supervisor, a first baseman; to the teacher, a learner of arithmetic. At times, he may be different things to each of these specialists, but too rarely is he a whole child to any of them.

— From the 1930 report of the White House Conference on Children and Youth, cited in Harold Hodgkinson, *The Same Client: The Demographics of Education and Service Delivery Systems*, 1989.

Ricardo and his family are being "served" by at least nine agencies— but no one agency truly takes responsibility for helping Ricardo, and separately they fail to treat him as a whole person. They are paid to treat each of a variety of "problems"—poor grades or absenteeism or child abuse, for instance—that add up to his being at risk. And they have no way to get beyond these symptoms to who he is as a whole person, and so he moves, lost, from one agency to another.

— From "Failure by Fragmentation" by Sid Gardner, Fall 1989.

**TABLE 1**  Examples of Types of Collaborative Activities

| Level | Activity |
| --- | --- |
| Service delivery | Case management: a worker collaborates personally with a range of other service deliverers in order to provide a broad menu of services to a family. |
| | Case management within a structure of formal interagency agreements that guarantee access to resources. |
| | Team staffings, to ensure that information is shared and decisions made jointly about individual cases. |
| | Colocation of services, one-stop shopping. |
| | Cross-training among service deliverers. |
| | Regular team meetings of service deliverers from multiple agencies, to share information and perspectives on the system as a whole, not just individual cases. |
| | Regular team meetings within a structure in which the service deliverers at the meeting have authority to change policies. |
| Program | Interagency agreements specifying access to resources, joint roles of staff. |
| | Flexibility to use resources across program boundaries. |
| | Changes in policies or structures to respond to needs identified by other systems, improve access, etc. |
| | Regular meetings by program directors to discuss policies, needs of target populations, quality of services, etc. |
| | Sharing of information about populations served. |
| | Joint efforts at intake and case tracking. |
| | Joint decisions about target populations to be served and services to be offered. |
| Community or city | Joint information collection about families, neighborhoods, and services. |
| | Joint development of mission statement and accountability measures. |
| | Joint decisions or recommendations about allocation of resources or at least priorities for new programs. |
| State or federal | Policy changes or waivers to produce pooled funding streams for local programs, probably with conditions for inclusiveness and accountability of local efforts. |
| | Joint development of accountability measures. |
| | Changes in regulation to eliminate major barriers to collaboration. |
| | Grant funding made available with incentives to collaboration, or on condition of collaboration. |
| | Mandates for joint planning. |
| | Joint information collection about families and services, joint planning, joint development of priorities for resource allocation or for new programs. |
| | Technical assistance to communities, cities, programs, service delivery workers to carry out all the new collaborative activities. |
| | Dissemination of information about collaborative activities. |
| Academic institution | Development of joint curricula, across social work, education, public health, mental health. |

These two quotations 60 years apart point to exactly the same problem: a fragmented service system that fails to serve a child as a whole person, let alone a family as a whole unit. If anything, it looks as though the problem has gotten worse from the first to the second: at least the first child is seen by two of the service deliverers as someone with capacities, while the second child is seen solely as someone with problems.

Why so little success over all that time? Many authors have identified a long list of reasons why collaboration is difficult in the world of child and family services (see for example Schorr, 1988; Weissbourd, 1990; Gardner, 1989; Weiss, 1981):

• *Categorical funding streams.* Federal and state funding sources tend to support programs defined in terms of substantive categoriesSecond, multiple governmental jurisdictions, and therefore multiple accountability relationsheriment with collaboration in child welfare, the state put together what had originally been 30 different funding streams.

• *Professional education and traditions.* Teachers, social workers, pediatricians, mental health clinicians, and all the rest of the service deliverers for children and families have had different educational backgrounds, speak different languages, and look to their own professions for recognition, respect, and promotion.

• *Organizational rigidities and loyalties.* Reinforcing the professional loyalties are organizational loyalties that may lead staff to view other agencies suspiciously: they have an easy job or don't really care about children the way we do, for example. At the same time, staff may well be trained and monitored for their conformity to rigid organizational procedures, which cannot be varied to meet the needs of other agencies or of families who don't fit the categories. For example, one welfare agency did not succeed in collaborating with an early childhood development program because it monitored its workers for attention to "mandatory" enrollees in work and training—whose youngest child was at least six—rather than "voluntary" enrollees, who might have a child the right age for the early childhood program (Golden, 1990: 133-139).

• *Inadequate resources to do the core job.* As suggested above, collaboration has costs, which staff may be unable or unwilling to incur if they cannot carry out their core functions well. While it may be true over the long term that collaboration will help solve core problems, individual workers may not be in a position to take a chance in the short term. For example, when child welfare workers are stretched to their limit to investigate emergency cases, even simple collaborative activities like explaining to school personnel why they are unable to take action on an abuse and neglect referral seem impossible—and more demanding activities such as meeting with teachers to talk about common concerns can't even be contemplated.[2]

But this list of problems seems to me to raise another question: why, over 30 years or more, haven't we been able to solve them? Surely with a compelling analysis of the benefits of collaboration, we ought to have been able to make funding streams more flexible, break down the barriers of professional education and organizational rigidity, and persuade workers and administrators that core functions will be advanced, not hindered, by work with other agencies.

The answer, I think, is that once again we cannot ignore the costs of collaboration or the benefits of the existing structure, the values that all of these barriers and obstacles are protecting. In particular, two important values protected by a fragmented system are differentiated expertise and accountability for functions that the public and political leaders know, understand, and believe in. If we are to develop recommendations for collaboration that can survive, we need to take these values seriously.

### The Value of Differentiated Expertise

The definition of collaboration offered above emphasized that it involves different organizations with their own different outlooks and purposes. As many writers have noted (see for example Lawrence and Lorsch, 1967), this differentiation of mission, expertise, and outlook among organizations (or even parts of organizations) is precisely what makes it difficult to work together. At the same time, this differentiation is there for a reason: the different organizations are responding to different technologies, different environments, different problems. A terrific surgeon can't work in exactly the same way as a terrific classroom teacher: the tasks are too different, and so the approach is different. An organization made up of terrific surgeons will, as a result, operate quite differently from an organization made up of terrific classroom teachers.

But what do you do when it is important for organizations that are legitimately very differentiated to work together in order to accomplish a crucial purpose? A famous study of private-sector corporations argues that this is precisely the situation in certain industries characterized by rapidly changing technologies, markets, and production and a need for constant and innovative response. In these industries, success requires high levels of both differentiation (that is, specialized expertise in very different fields—for example, in basic research and customer relations) *and* integration (that is, collaboration to further the common mission of the firm). The study argues

---

[2]For this experience from the teacher's point of view, see Weissbourd (1989).

that although there is a trade-off between differentiation and integration; excellent companies achieve a higher level of both than weaker companies, relying on a variety of techniques to improve communication and resolve conflicts (Lawrence and Lorsch, 1967:52-53).

The implication for collaborative services to children and families, it seems to me, is that we may be in exactly the same position as companies in those difficult industries: our success, at least for the most needy children, may depend on excellence at both differentiation and integration. That is, more than other children, the most fragile children may need skilled teachers, counselors, and sometimes even surgeons—yet at the same time, more than other children, they need to be helped by these skilled specialists as whole children, seen in the light of other aspects of their lives. To take a slightly different example, responding successfully to the needs of a fragile family with a very ill baby may require both the highly differentiated skills of the surgeon and the ability to integrate many different services around the family's needs.

Thus, to think effectively about collaboration, we may need to think about differentiation and maintaining separate standards of excellence at the same time. As I argue below, effective collaborations seem to take up this challenge in two ways: they try to redefine the mission of each constituent unit to some degree, in order to make vivid to each specialist how he or she fits into the overall picture, and they also anticipate continuing conflict even with the redefined missions and develop effective ways of resolving it.

### The Value of Accountability

Besides the inherent value of differentiated expertise, public-sector agencies also need to take into account their political mandate. Public agencies are accountable to political overseers and ultimately to the public, who have a conception, implicit or explicit, of what those agencies are supposed to be doing. In many cases, public conceptions are defined in terms of the differentiated missions, not the integrated ones. Therefore, shifting toward collaboration may look to the public and the political overseers like shifting toward activities on the fringe of the agency's mission, at the expense of the core. For example, child protective agencies are expected by the public to prevent children from injury and death and to place children in safe foster homes that will not endanger them further. Public welfare agencies are expected to control the total amount of money they spend and spend it accurately. The director of one welfare agency that has engaged in successful collaboration reports that he is able to spend his time on external tasks only because his agency has a history of excellence on cost control, fraud control, and automation that gives him the freedom to move outward.

Two features of accountability in the field of children's services may further complicate the task of the agency trying to move to a broader mission. First, the narrow missions may well be much easier to measure in quantitative terms: it is, for example, easy to measure how accurately the welfare department is determining eligibility. Without equivalent benchmarks for the new, broader mission, the public may be suspicious, and the "harder" measurements may tend to drive out the fuzzier or harder-to-measure mission from the minds of agency workers and managers.

Second, multiple governmental jurisdictions, and therefore multiple accountability relationships, characterize services to children and families in the United States. The agencies we might select to collaborate around services to families and children are generally accountable not to one but to two, three, or four different levels of government or elected bodies. Welfare and child protective services are generally located at the state or county level; the school system is likely to be more local, possibly but not necessarily coterminous with the city or county government and probably accountable to a separately elected school board; the city government may fund a variety of child and family services; Head Start programs are subgrantees to the federal government; and so forth. In one California county with an impressive record on collaboration, the collaborating agencies worked for four separate governmental jurisdictions: the city, the county, the unified school district, and the community college district. That list does not include the state and federal governments, which provided funds for major services such as welfare and child welfare and therefore demanded accountability to their own rules and purposes.

The important point here is that accountability for an agency's purposes and effectiveness is not in itself a villain; it is part of a democratic system. But left to themselves, many of our existing mechanisms for accountability will operate against collaboration and for existing bureaucratic procedures. Effective collaboration, therefore, requires the deployment of political, analytic, and managerial talent to discover and carry out alternative approaches to accountability (see also Gardner, 1989; Morrill and Gerry, no date).

## ELEMENTS OF SUCCESSFUL COLLABORATION

With that range of barriers, it seems extraordinary that recent reports identify so many collaborations on behalf of families and children that have been successful at least for some period of time. How do these successful collaborations overcome the range of barriers described above?

Based on the programs that I have studied, supplemented by an incomplete review of the literature, I would offer two general answers. First, we should not forget that, although we can identify many successes, we can also identify many programs that don't succeed. For example, in the research on welfare and children's services, out of seven programs we selected for study because of their professional reputation as successes, two are no longer operating as collaborations, only a year after our site visits (Golden, 1990).[3] The implication I draw from this point is not that we should give up but that we should understand what success in promoting collaborative service provision really means: creating an atmosphere where *more*, but still not all, attempts at collaboration could succeed over the long run.

Second and perhaps more optimistically, the successful collaborations, while sharing many common themes, demonstrate a particular knack for skillful adaptation to their local situations. While they must overcome a common set of barriers and address some number of a common set of tasks, their success at overcoming the barriers and completing the tasks comes precisely from their ability to adapt to local characteristics and needs. For example, collaborations are able to develop a common mission despite the pressure for differentiated, specialized missions precisely because the collaborators are good at identifying important local problems that require cross-cutting activities for their solution.

More specifically, in the remainder of this section, I identify five common elements of successful collaboration that come out of my own research on welfare agencies and children's services and that appear consistent with other findings in the literature. I add a sixth element that is frequently mentioned in the literature and seems centrally related to the underlying justification for collaboration.

(1) *Redefined and overlapping missions.* Collaborating organizations have succeeded in developing overlapping conceptions of mission. They have managed to enlarge their missions beyond the conventional limits associated with their agency, often because of managerial skill in identifying key local political problems or opportunities.

(2) *Conflict resolution.* In effective collaborations, people do not expect that conflict between the organizations will disappear or attribute such conflict solely to uncooperative personalities, power struggles, or turf battles. Instead, they develop ongoing mechanisms for conflict resolution.

(3) *Commitment of managerial time.* Managers devote considerable time and attention to collaboration, spending time looking out from their organizations rather than simply up or down within them.

(4) *Role of personal relationships.* Managers and service deliverers cultivate personal relationships as a basis for collaboration.

(5) *Exchange relationships.* Collaborating agencies have some basis for exchange—something they can do for each other.

(6) *Involvement of families and a broad spectrum of the community.* A number of writers have argued that involvement of those who are served at all stages of the collaboration—from planning to service delivery—is critical to success.

---

[3]See Weiss (1981:24) for a pessimistic assessment of the failure rate of collaborations.

### Redefined and Overlapping Missions

If one explanation for the difficulty of collaboration is agencies' differentiated missions, we might expect to see redefined and overlapping missions in successful collaborations. Several recent reviews of collaborative experience have developed this theme: for example, one recent report emphasizes the role of establishing values and sharing a vision, and another notes the value of overlapping administrative responsibilities and legal mandates (see for example Institute for Educational Leadership, no date; Levy, 1989).

The evidence from seven sites I studied at which the welfare agency collaborated in the delivery of children's services is consistent with this theme. For example, a collaboration between a welfare agency and a nonprofit agency providing child care resource and referral services to welfare recipients illustrates a common conception of mission. In our interviews, eligibility workers and employment and training (ET) workers at the welfare department and parent counselors at the child care resource and referral agency told stories about their own aims and their own greatest successes that suggested a common mission: self-sufficiency for mothers on welfare, coupled with excellent child care to ensure a mother's peace of mind.

The sites also illustrate the other side of this proposition: in cases in which the mission conflicts have not been effectively resolved, collaboration has not succeeded. For example, we visited a program in which the welfare agency was funding several sites in a family literacy program that provided a high school equivalency program for the parent and a preschool program for the child, with slots at those collaborative sites to be reserved for welfare recipients. The agencies began the project because it seemed to meet both their needs: the family literacy program had difficulty recruiting families, and the welfare department was interested in training programs for mothers, particularly given the convenient pairing with child care. But the collaboration did not survive early difficulties, because the local welfare office saw its primary mission as following the rules on benefit checks and processing clients who were mandated to register for training programs. Because the families with young children who were appropriate for the family literacy program were not mandated registrants, welfare workers did not refer enough families to fill the program, and local office administrators were unable to move beyond their mission and improvise an agreement to solve the problem. Although intervention from the welfare agency's central office filled the program in its first year, the welfare agency chose not to participate again in the second year.

But how do agencies develop support for a broader sense of mission, given the pressure for narrower accountability described above? The answer suggested by the sites I studied is consistent with that suggested by several recent reports: successful collaborations are extremely responsive to local needs, to problems already defined or potentially definable by the local political system. As Levy (1989) points out, "systemic pain," meaning problems that no one can solve alone, is a powerful source of collaboration (see also Institute for Educational Leadership, no date). One of the collaborative managers in a site I studied expresses his belief that this motivation will eventually drive widespread collaboration (Golden, 1990:11):

> Economics are going to drive it. They will force people to get together. Everyone around the country has overwhelming caseloads and too few resources. The Federal deficit won't be resolved, taxes won't be enough to keep up with health and social problems. So collaboration makes sense from an economic point of view.

But the nature of the "systemic pain" that drove collaboration in my study sites, and the mission that emerged from that pain, did not seem to me to be consistent across collaborations. Rather, agency managers were able to take advantage of particular political and organizational opportunities to develop their own unique problem and mission definition. The agencies have sustained political and organizational support through a match between the precise form of the collaborative mission and locally defined problems and needs. For example, a Detroit program involving collaboration between the welfare agency and the schools responded to local concern about school dropouts, a problem that was politically salient there in a way that "losing families between the cracks," one of the problems that drives another of the site programs, might not be (Golden, 1990:147-157).

## Conflict Resolution

Defining collaboration as the effort to integrate units that must at the same time remain highly differentiated makes sharply evident the need for continuing processes of conflict resolution in even the most successful collaboration. Teachers, psychiatrists, and child protective workers will inevitably see different aspects of a child, no matter how respectful they are of each other's viewpoints, and some mechanism for settling the disagreements seems critical. Perhaps because of an idealized view of collaboration, this aspect has not been much studied, although several reports emphasize the value of skilled facilitators to collaborations, and one report notes that a mechanism for "voicing concerns" is crucial to successful collaborations.[4] This finding is similar to the Lawrence and Lorsch (1967) finding in the private sector that effective conflict resolution in highly differentiated

---

[4]The phrase "voicing concerns" is from Institute for Educational Leadership (no date: 42-44.) One source in which the facilitator suggestion is developed at length is Robinson and Mastny (1989).

organizations involved more direct and explicit disagreement than ineffective conflict resolution.

Again, the findings from my sites are consistent with the idea that effective conflict resolution matters to collaboration. For example, although ET workers and parent counselors in the child care agency agree on their broad mission, they reported disagreeing on priorities for particular families. For example, the parent counselors reported that they might disagree with ET workers about the timing of a mother's entry into training: Should she start right away, or should she wait until the next program cycle to take the time to feel more comfortable with her child care arrangements? They reported a clear sense of how they would resolve that conflict: they would encourage the client to delay (which she is able to do under a voluntary program), speak to the ET worker if necessary, and perhaps try to "educate" workers at the public welfare office as a whole about the nature of adjustment to child care.

One of the other sites at which the collaboration has dissolved seemed to have a particularly ineffective mechanism for conflict resolution. In this collaboration, between a nonprofit organization and a county department of social services, there was no clear process for resolving conflicts that might have been easily anticipated, given the agencies' different missions and purposes. Conflicts appeared to drag on, without personal meetings or negotiation, and to be elevated through exchanges of high-level memos and sometimes testimony at public or legislative hearings.

## Commitment of Managerial Time

In the sites I studied, the program managers in successful collaborations devote enormous time and attention to collaboration—to facing outward from their organization rather than merely up or down within it. For example, the founder of the San Diego Teen Parent Project reports that her proudest achievement from the program's first year was its strong reputation in the community, and she continues to reserve considerable time to meet with outside organizations, including a regular monthly meeting with two other agencies that focus on teenagers. Her advice to other jurisdictions is to make sure you have linkages to other organizations first. Similarly, the program director of a teenage parent program in New York State describes her long-standing and constructive relationships with a wide variety of community service providers as key in getting services to clients, and she says that "We make it our business to know how to get in the back door." At the service delivery level as well, caseworkers in many of the programs report a great deal of time spent in contact with other providers, ranging from formalized roles as on-site liaison to other agencies and convener of "team staffings" to less structured roles in other case management programs.

This finding, that successful collaborators spend a lot of time and energy on collaboration, is not generally reported in quite this form, perhaps because it seems too obvious. But it is consistent with the process-oriented and clearly time-consuming approaches to collaboration recommended by a number of sources and with the exhortation not to expect immediate results (Levy, 1989:16). It is also consistent with the idea that successful collaborations have to be good at both differentiation and integration: one way to do better at both sides of a trade-off is to invest a great deal of managerial time and energy.

## Role of Personal Relationships

The site visits I conducted are consistent with another finding widely reported in the literature on collaboration and case management: that "institutions don't collaborate, people do" (Toby Herr, cited in Bruner, 1990b). That is, collaboration in the sites is associated with a network of personal relationships, built over time, between the major participants. Staff in the successful collaborations make a special effort to select strategies with a personal element: for example, face-to-face meetings instead of communications by phone or memo and colocation or outstationing of workers whenever possible so that people get to know each other. Among the examples of successful techniques using this approach:

• In San Diego, the heads of the GAIN Teen Parent Program, the major health center for pregnant teens, and the major community case management program meet in person once a month for a formal meeting and see each other informally much more often. As a result, the head of the health center describes their relationship as "much stronger than simply referrals . . . much more personal."

• In Oklahoma, one local Integrated Family Services case manager says that at first he doubted the value of the face-to-face meetings of service deliverers that the state requires him to convene, because he already talked to them frequently on the phone. He now thinks the meetings are important, because "face-to-face is different."

In two instances of collaboration that did not last in the sites, personal links seem to have been missing:

• In the site mentioned earlier with weak conflict resolution between the community nonprofit and the county social services department, the relationship did not involve frequent personal contacts at the case manager level; at the time we were there, problems were being addressed through memos between the program supervisors.

• In the collaboration between the family literacy program and the welfare department, there was personal contact and collaboration at the state level but considerably less at the site level. At the time we were there, the literacy teachers reported having visited the welfare department once, but most communication seemed to be over the phone about particular problems.

## Exchange Relationships

A number of reports on successful collaborations describe what the agencies are able to do for each other: for example, school-based collaborations typically offer outside agencies access to children they could not otherwise reach (see for example Petit, 1988; Sylvester, 1990). My sites suggest that, although the particulars of the exchange depend on the substantive domains of the agencies and their local environments, successful collaborations seem often to involve skill at creating exchanges, at noticing what one agency can do for another. In Oklahoma, when an Integrated Family Services (IFS) unit was first set up in a community to work with multineed families who might be falling through gaps in the system, the IFS case managers did not simply announce they were there to coordinate other service deliverers. Instead, they spent several months learning how they could offer concrete assistance that would build their credibility, for example by developing an automated resource directory and identifying training and service gaps they might be able to fill. In Detroit, a dropout prevention program run by the department of social services demonstrated in its first two years that it could meet specific needs of the schools— assistance in keeping kids in school, a capacity for home visits and connection to families, an ability to run interference in the bureaucracy—and the schools have responded with a commitment of resources for the planned expansion.

Although there are common themes to the exchanges, there is also considerable local variation. An exchange that works for one school district or family services agency will not work for another, because the agencies' needs, the key problems they are focused on, and their resources are different. One school district may be eager to serve teenage parents and want to work with the welfare department around case management services and child care for them; another district may face resistance from citizens who view teenage pregnancy as someone else's problem and may therefore be more willing to work on reaching families whose children are in middle school. The structure of Oklahoma's IFS explicitly recognizes this multiplicity of needs in the agencies with which the welfare department needs to cooperate, by leaving great flexibility to the local IFS teams to identify needs and develop particular roles to meet those needs. Programs we heard about ranged from a rural site where the biggest issue is farm families in crisis to an urban site where a local community group wants the help of an IFS team to carry out health and housing-related projects. The state IFS director viewed both projects as consistent with the IFS focus on community capacity to serve troubled families with multiple needs.

## Involvement of Families

Several writers emphasize the importance of including those who will receive services in the collaboration. Gardner (1989), for example, argues that effective collaborations can only come out of broad-based community planning efforts. Bruner (1990b) argues persuasively for the role of collaboration between family and service deliverer as the foundation for broader collaboration. If, as I have argued above, the whole reason for collaboration in programs to serve at-risk families and children is founded in the needs and characteristics of those families, then it makes sense that effective collaborations would have to go back over and over to those families to make sure they were in fact in line with real needs.

## NOTES TOWARD SOME RECOMMENDATIONS

Having suggested that collaboration occurs in many different ways at many different levels, that it is extremely difficult, and that successful collaborations overcome those difficulties through ingenious local adaptations, I am not in a position to offer authoritative recommendations. The challenge I have left for myself (and the group) is to identify recommendations that are not so small in scope or incremental as to produce trivial effects and yet not so sweeping as to contradict the arguments offered above about the complex and essentially local nature of collaboration. Therefore, I have tried to select recommendations that influence large parts of the service system by changing the capacities, resources, or incentives of those within it, rather than by prescribing narrow models. I have also tried to select arenas in which the recommendations of a group like the forum might carry particular weight.

Based on these criteria, I propose four recommendations as a starting point for discussion:

(1) Academic institutions should develop curricula across the professional specialties for street-level service deliverers (social workers, teachers, doctors, nurses) that prepare them for collaboration, as well as in-service training for supervisors, program managers, and high-level administrators.

One advantage of this recommendation is that we in academia can work on it ourselves, rather than only exhorting others to act. It also fits the multiple and local nature of the tasks involved in collaboration: rather than prescribing rigid models, we could support those involved in collaboration in developing the skills to create their own models.

(2) States and the federal government should experiment with pooled funding streams and new accountability measures.

Sid Gardner has proposed that state governments (after negotiating federal waivers) could decategorize a wide range of funding streams for selected localities. That is, the states could pool the money and offer localities the opportunity to spend the whole lump sum for the purpose of improving the lives of families and children, with complete discretion over how best to spend it to meet local needs (Gardner, 1990). The conditions for this offer would be an inclusive local planning process, probably with signoff by the important local interests and outcome measures agreed to by the community. The closest thing to a real example of this is probably Iowa's experiment with decategorizing child welfare funding in selected counties (Bruner, 1990a).

(3) States and cities should experiment with partnerships in which the city takes responsibility for services to children and the state agrees to support that responsibility. More concretely, the city would convene citizens to determine what the current service picture looks like, what the needs are, and what should change; the state would agree to help with identified needs (regulatory waivers, funding shifts, training and technical assistance, etc.).

This is a variant on the previous plan that is not as dependent on freeing up large amounts of money from restrictions right away. The experience of cities that have developed children's policies (like Minneapolis and Seattle) or that are currently developing them (like Cambridge, Mass.) suggests that when mayors are eager to take some level of responsibility for children's outcomes, we should encourage their interest even if they control only a small part of service delivery, because of the critical role they can play in convening and influencing a community-wide process.

(4) Advocates and policy makers within each of the relevant children's services fields should seize upcoming legislative opportunities to encourage thinking and implementation across substantive boundaries.

For example, the implementation of the Family Support Act, the likely implementation of the Act for Better Child Care, and the likely consideration over the next few years of new child welfare legislation offer opportunities to think about how best to build in collaboration.

## CONCLUSION

Collaboration is an appealing strategy for improving services to poor children and families, but it is clearly not an easy strategy. To the extent that many teachers, nurses, social workers, school principals and superintendents, health clinic directors, welfare office managers, and state agency heads are concluding on their own that they cannot do their jobs without it, the timing may be right for efforts to support and channel the stream of collaborative experiments so that they will be most effective, most influential, and most likely to last. And, if enough experiments get started, supported from enough different levels at the same time, so that communities truly change the way they serve families, then the experience of success could create a powerful momentum for further change. As Director Richard Jacobsen of the San Diego County Department of Social Services argues, there is a certain simple power to the common mission that agencies can arrive at when they realize they are serving the same clients: "to eliminate patients, clients, offenders and increase the number of leaders, parents, students."

## ACKNOWLEDGMENT

This paper draws in part on research on welfare agencies and services to children funded by the Foundation for Child Development. It also draws heavily on the conversations and working papers of the Kennedy School of Government's Executive Session on Making the System Work for Poor Children, funded by the Carnegie Foundation. I want to thank all the members of the executive session for their ideas, which I have probably borrowed here. I want to thank particularly those who have written down their ideas, including Mary Jo Bane, Charles Bruner, Sid Gardner, Paul Jargowsky, and Rick Weissbourd. The interpretations, conclusions, and recommendations, though, are mine and do not claim to reflect the views of other members.

## REFERENCES

Bruner, Charles
    1991a State-Level Approaches to Foster Local-Level Collaboration: Iowa's Initiatives to Improve Children's Welfare. Unpublished paper prepared for NCSL. July.
    1990b Twelve Questions State Policy Makers Should Ask About Fostering Collaboration in Meeting Children's Needs. Unpublished manuscript prepared for the William T. Grant Foundation. July 31.
Gardner, Sid
    1989 Failure by fragmentation. *California Tomorrow* (Fall):20-21.
    1990 The Hugo System: A Storm That Might Blow Children Some Good. Unpublished paper prepared for the Executive Session on Making the System Work for Poor Children. January.
Golden, Olivia, with Mary Skinner and Ruth Baker
    1990 Welfare Reform and Poor Children: Collaboration and Case Management Approaches. Draft final report prepared for the Foundation for Child Development. September.
Institute for Educational Leadership
    no    What It Takes: Comprehensive Service Delivery Through School
    date  and Human Service Collaborations. Unpublished paper.

Lawrence, Paul R., and Jay W. Lorsch

1967 *Organization and Environment: Managing Differentiation and Integration.* Boston: Division of Research, Graduate School of Business Administration, Harvard University.

Levy, Janet E., with Carol Copple

1989 *Joining Forces: A Report From the First Year.* Alexandria, Va.: National Association of State Boards of Education.

Morrill, William A., and Martin H. Gerry

no Integrating the Delivery of Services to School-Aged Children at
date Risk. Unpublished paper prepared for the U.S. Department of Education, Conference on Children and Youth at Risk.

Petit, Michael

1988 Issues Surrounding State-Level Collaboration on Services to At-Risk, Preschool Age Children. Paper presented to the Summer Institute of the Council of Chief State School Officers. August.

Robinson, Estelle R., and Aleta You Mastny

1989 Linking Schools and Community Services: A Practical Guide. Center for Community Education, School of Social Work, Rutgers University.

Schorr, Lisbeth, with Daniel Schorr

1988 *Within Our Reach: Breaking the Cycle of Disadvantage.* New York: Doubleday/Anchor Press.

Sylvester, Kathleen

1990 New strategies to save children in trouble. *Governing* (May):32-37.

Weiss, Janet A.

1981 Substance vs. symbol in administration reform: The case of human services coordination. *Policy Analysis* (Winter):20-45.

Weissbourd, Rick

1989 Public Elementary Schools: A Ladder Out of Poverty? Unpublished paper prepared for the Executive Session on Making the System Work for Poor Children. October.

1990 Making the System Work for Poor Children. Unpublished paper prepared for the Executive Session on Making the System Work for Poor Children. October.

# Outcomes as a Tool to Provoke Systems Change

*David W. Hornbeck*
Education Adviser, Baltimore, Md.

I wish to begin this brief paper with three observations. First, the condition of children is deteriorating. The relationship of that fact to the nation's economic prowess and to our ability to function as a democracy when the wealth gap is widening is increasing the stakes attached to success in our human service systems. As a result, the pressure from many quarters to provide greater productivity is growing rapidly.

Second, the citizenry, according to every poll, appears to be willing to pay a larger bill. *But only if it results in improvement.* The public does not believe that business as usual will do the job. A paradigm shift must occur. To use education to illustrate, the greatest proportion of the students with whom the system fails most miserably are in our cities. We have a poor record in the states with respect to fiscal equity much less fiscal adequacy for cities. Reapportionment based on the census will generally weaken the political power of cities, not strengthen it. Thus, more than ever before, greater resources will depend on our convincing legislators at the state and federal level that new increases will be significantly more productive than previous increases. An outcome-based system can provide that assurance since it embodies real consequence associated with the achievement of results.

Third, because the paradigm recommended below shifts responsibility and authority closer to the students (clients, patients, participants), there is less incentive to wait for someone at a central level to tell the staff at the grass-roots level what to do. Therefore, the proportion of people in the system seeking successful solutions can increase dramatically. The incentives and disincentives are rearrayed so that teachers, social workers, and health professionals in local neighborhoods are less constrained and are *expected* to find solutions and produce. In education, for example, that means answers and effort not from just 50 state superintendents and 16,000 local superintendents but from 90,000 principals and 2,000,000 teachers as well. That is a hugh increase in professional wisdom targeted by the selected outcomes resulting in consequences.

In the pages that follow, although the generic principles are applicable to all human service systems, I shall use education as the vehicle to illustrate several points since it is the system I know best. Moreover, in several places, I illustrate points with recommendations from legislation recently passed in Kentucky, the only place of which I am aware that has embraced an aggressive outcome-based initiative related to a human service system.

Within public education, the primary question governing the system is, "Did you do what they told you to do?" Sometimes it is asked directly of school staff. More often it is reflected in the forms that all levels of government ask the levels below to fill out . It is embedded in the culture of public schooling, reflected, for example, in the observation of too many teachers overheard to say, "I taught them; they just didn't learn it."

The right question is "Did it work?" Trying hard must no longer suffice as a standard of performance. Results must control practice. Can the student(s) read and comprehend? Can the class "do" science at the level expected? Have the students attained foreign language proficiency? And so on.

Increasingly, we are seeing such an outcome orientation emerging in public education. The national goals and underlying objectives adopted by the President and the governors last winter emphasize that. The President's Education Advisory Committee is moving toward a national examination. The National Education Goals Panel chaired by Governor Romer of Colorado is to issue an annual report card on the states. The Congress is seriously considering at least one bill that would establish a similar report card panel. The Business Roundtable, comprised of the nation's 200 largest corporations has made a 10-year commitment to a partnership with each of the 50 states to change the process and product of education. The centerpiece of their public policy agenda is an outcome-based strategy. Kentucky has already legislated an aggressive outcome strategy. Other states are presently considering such an approach.

A comprehensive outcomes-based strategy is essential to provoke the degree of systems change necessary to yield the results we desire. There are at least seven essential features of an outcomes based approach.

First, one must examine the underlying assumptions that provide the lens through which one will identify the outcomes to be achieved. In education, two are crucial. The first is the assumption that all children can learn at very significantly higher levels. Expectation becomes a self-fulfilling prophecy. The second assumption is that we know how to teach successfully children from all backgrounds to those significantly higher levels.

The second essential feature is to identify the outcomes one expects the system to produce with all students (clients, patients, participants). If low expectation outcomes are identified, that will inevitably define the results; if high expectation outcomes are identified, students, staff and the community will more likely achieve them. In Kentucky, 10 outcomes areas were picked:

- Communication and math skills;
- Students' ability to apply core concepts and principles from mathematics, the sciences, the arts, the humanities, social studies, and practical living studies;
- Self-sufficiency (physical and mental fitness, creativity, ethical decision making);
- Citizenship (team member, service, values, other cultures);
- Thinking and problem solving;
- Connecting and integrating knowledge;
- Dropout reduction;
- Attendance increase;
- Healthier students; and
- Postgraduation success.

Each of these areas is being defined in terms of indicators so that their attainment can be measured.

The third essential feature of an outcomes-based system is that one must have assessment strategies that are as rich as the outcomes one wishes to achieve. Outcomes that cannot be or are not measured will soon become irrelevant. If high expectation outcomes such as knowledge application, thinking, problem solving and knowledge
integration are to be emphasized assessment strategies such as performance based assessment, essays, portfolios, and student projects will become more prominent.

The fourth essential feature is that there must be consequence attached to a system's success or failure in achieving results with its students (clients, patients, participants). Incentives and disincentives related to performance by schools should become routine. The reward and penalties must be designed to ensure that those the system is to serve are helped and not harmed. Parts of the system that fail should be helped to improve, not simply punished. Success must be carefully defined to avoid unintended negative consequences. In Kentucky, with certain very good results a school staff could receive as much as 40 percent of annual salary as a bonus. At the other extreme, staff in a school that is losing substantial ground with it students could have tenure suspended, resulting in dismissal. Unsuccessful schools are eligible for school improvement funds, technical assistance, special access to staff development, and research-based instructional activities. In Kentucky, the school is the unit of measurement; "success" reflects student performance on the outcomes outlined above; a school's performance is measured only against itself.

The fifth essential feature of an outcomes-based system is that those who are closest to the student (client, patient, participant) who are held accountable for achieving the outcomes must have the power to decide what strategies will be used to accomplish the objectives. In Kentucky, school staffs augmented by parents will select personnel, make budget decisions, select curriculum and instructional materials, decide on the school schedule, assign teachers and students within the school, and adopt the disciplinary code. In a variety of ways the central office and the school board also play an important role in these decisions, but school-based personnel are not merely consulted; they have real authority.

The sixth essential feature is that those who must achieve the outcomes and be held accountable in a high stakes way must be educated to have the capacity to do so. In education that means significant changes in both preservice and in-service training.

The seventh essential feature of an outcomes-based system is that certain enabling conditions must exist if significantly high results are to achieved with *all* students (clients, patients, participants). High-expectation outcomes cannot occur without defining them, but they will not occur by that act alone. The enabling conditions in Kentucky include: prekindergarten for all disadvantaged students; a family resource center in every elementary school with 20 percent or more poor children; ungraded primary schools; a $200 million technology initiative; the fiscal capacity for one-third of the children to go to school the equivalent of year round.

What I have described is an outcomes-based *system*. I would argue that all seven features are essential. If one is removed, 86 percent of the effort does *not* remain; 0 percent remains.

I have used education in general and Kentucky in particular to illustrate the points. However, I believe the essential features are generic and applicable to human service systems other than education as well. The generic features in summary are: (a) assumptions; (b) outcome definition; (c) adequate assessment; (d) rewards and penalties; (e) site-based decision making; (f) staff development; (g) enabling conditions. Clearly, it will require a change in thinking and structures (as is required in education too) but the health and social service systems should be equally susceptible to change provoked by the same features.

APPENDIX

# Workshop Agenda and Participants

# WORKSHOP ON EFFECTIVE SERVICES
# FOR YOUNG CHILDREN

## November 1-2, 1990

FIRST DAY, NOVEMBER 1

10:00 - 10:10    WELCOME - Julius Richmond, Chair
National Forum on the Future of Children and Families

10:10 - Noon    *Session I: Attributes of Effective Services*

*Chair:* Mary Jo Bane, Kennedy School of Government, Harvard University

*Objective:* To examine the level of consensus among researchers, policy analysts, and practitioners regarding the common attributes of successful programs for high-risk children and their families and to achieve some agreement among participants around the most crucial, common attributes.

*Paper:* Lisbeth B. Schorr, Harvard University

*Discussants:* Rosalie Street, Friends of the Family, Incorporated; Sister Mary Paul Janchill, Center for Family Life in Sunset Park; Robert Granger, Manpower Demonstration Research Corporation

Noon - 1:00    LUNCH

1:00 - 2:45    *Session II: Lessons from Earlier Efforts*

*Chair:* Lisle Carter, United Way of America

*Objective:* To review and extract lessons from major federal and state efforts of the last 25 years, such as the Model Cities Program, community action programs, block grants, etc., which were designed to improve coordination, reduce fragmentation, and ensure greater accessibility to services.

*Paper:* Peter Edelman, Georgetown University Law School; Beryl Radin, Washington Public Affairs Center, University of Southern California

*Discussants:* Douglas Besharov, American Enterprise Institute for Public Policy Research; Robert Greenstein, Center on Budget and Policy Priorities

2:45 - 3:00 BREAK

3:00 - 5:15     *Session IIIA: Strategies for Implementing Change*

*Objective:* To identify and assess strategies to promote the widespread adoption and implementation of programs incorporating the attributes of successful programs.

All workshop participants will be assigned to partici-pate in one of the following two concurrent sessions:

1. *Strategies based on collaboration and coordination* (Room 150)

*Chair:* Janet Levy, Joining Forces

This session will consider collaboration and coordina-tion as strategies to promote the widespread adoption and implementation of effective programs. Topics to be addressed include: the purposes of collaboration, promis-ing processes, major obstacles, strategies for overcoming obstacles, common attributes of successful collaboration, and the extent to which generalizations can be made across communities, states, and systems.

*Paper:* Olivia Golden, Kennedy School of Government, Harvard University

*Discussants:* Martin Gerry, U.S. Department of Health and Human Services; Scott Fosler, Committee on Eco-nomic Development; Ralph Smith, Philadelphia Child-ren's Network; Tom Langfitt, Pew Charitable Trusts

2. *Financing strategies* (Room 250)

*Chair:* Richard Nathan, Nelson A. Rockefeller College of Public Affairs and Policy

This session will consider financing strategies to remove obstacles to—and provide incentives for—the provision of coherent effective services, including public and private efforts to combine funds from multiple existing sources, and efforts to change the way funds flow to local programs.

*Paper:* Frank Farrow, Center for the Study of Social Policy

*Discussants:* Drew Altman, Kaiser Family Foundation (Paper); Annette Abrams, Office of Children and Youth, Michigan

5:30 - 6:30  RECEPTION (Rotunda)

6:30 - 7:30  DINNER (Members Room)

7:30 - 9:00  *Session IV: Strategies Based on Building Greater Public Understanding of the Crucial Issues*

*Chair and Introductory Remarks:* James Comer, Yale University

This session will consider strategies to build greater public understanding of the crucial issues including: (a) the nature of the problem, (b) the societal stake in investing in promising solution, and (c) the nature of promising solutions.

*Discussants:* Kati Haycock, Children's Defense Fund Ann Rosewater, Consultant Robert Wehling, The Proctor & Gamble Company

## SECOND DAY, NOVEMBER 2

9:00 - 11:15  *Session IIIB: Strategies for Action (continued)*

All workshop participants will be assigned to participate in one of the following two concurrent sessions:

3. *Technical assistance and training strategies* (Room 150)

*Chair:* Barbara Blum, Foundation for Child Development

This session will consider technical assistance strategies to (a) assist managers in acquiring the requisite skills and expertise to manage reformed service programs, (b) provide a variety of agencies and institutions with help in training front-line workers to function effectively in reformed service programs, and (c) ensure that states and communities can obtain the training and technical assistance that would enable them to modify their operations, structures, funding patterns, etc., in ways that would encourage the development and survival of effective programs.

*Paper:* Doug Nelson, Annie E. Casey Foundation

*Discussants:* Charles Bruner, Child Family Policy Center Peter Forsythe, Edna McConnell Clark Foundation

4. *Strategies based on greater use of outcome measures* (Room 250)

*Chair:* Steve Kelman, Kennedy School of Government, Harvard University

This session will consider efforts to shift toward an outcome orientation to assure accountability, improve program performance, and provide the basis for investment of increased resources, allocated on more flexible terms.

*Paper:* David Hornbeck, Education Adviser, Baltimore, Md.

*Discussants:* Heather Weiss, Harvard Family Research Project; Sid Gardner, Youth at Risk Project

11:15 - 11:30  BREAK

11:30 - 4:00  *Session V: Making It Happen—Identifying Strategies for Systematic Change and Action* - Lunch will be provided (Lecture Room)

*Chair:* Harold Richman, Chapin Hall Center for Children, IL

*Objective:* Drawing on previous workshop discussions, to identify themes around which there seem to be some consensus; to integrate shared information and understanding in order to identify strategies that could result in systematic action to significantly improve services for high-risk children and their families, and to propose the agencies, institutions, or other entities that should be involved and responsible for the next steps.

*ADJOURN*

# PARTICIPANTS

Julius B. Richmond (Forum Chair), Division of Health Research and Education, Harvard University, Cambridge, MA

Lisbeth Schorr, (Workshop Chair), School of Medicine, Harvard University, Washington, DC

L. Annette Abrams, Office of Children and Youth Services, Lansing, MI

Drew Altman, Kaiser Family Foundation, Menlo Park, CA

Michael Bailin, Public/Private Ventures, Philadelphia, PA

Mary Jo Bane, John F. Kennedy School of Government, Harvard University, Cambridge, MA

Rhoda Baruch, Institute for Mental Health Initiatives, Washington, DC

Dennis Beatrice, Pew Charitable Trust, Philadelphia, PA

Douglas J. Besharov, American Enterprise Institute for Public Policy Research, Washington, DC

Martin Blank, Institute for Educational Leadership, Washington, DC

Barbara Blum, Foundation for Child Development, New York, NY

Prudence Brown, Urban Poverty Program, Ford Foundation, New York, NY

Charles Bruner, Child and Family Policy Center, Des Moines, IA

Michele Cahill, Academy for Educational Development, Inc., New York, NY

Lisle Carter, United Way of America, Alexandria, VA

James P. Comer, Child Study Center, Yale University, New Haven, CT

Gayle Dorman, Lilly Endowment Foundation, Indianapolis, IN

Peter Edelman, Georgetown University Law School, Washington, DC

Frank Farrow, Center for the Study of Social Policy, Washington, DC

Gilda Ferguson-Smith, Family Focus Lawndale, Chicago, IL

Peter Forsythe, Edna McConnell Clark Foundation, New York, NY

Scott Fosler, Committee on Economic Development, Washington, DC

Donald M. Fraser, Mayor, Minneapolis, MN

Sid Gardner, Youth at Risk Project, Orange, CA

Martin H. Gerry, Department of Health and Human Services, Washington, DC

Olivia Golden, John F. Kennedy School of Government, Cambridge, MA

Robert Granger, Manpower Demonstration Research Corporation, New York, NY

Robert Greenstein, Center on Budget and Policy Priorities, Washington, DC

Kati Haycock, Children's Defense Fund, Washington, DC

Fred M. Hechinger, New York Times Company Foundation, New York, NY

Wade Horn, Administration for Children, Youth and Families, Washington, DC

David W. Hornbeck, Education Adviser, Baltimore, MD

Sister Mary Paul Janchill, Center for Family Life in Sunset Park, Brooklyn, NY

Gloria Johnson-Powell, Camille Cosby Ambulatory Care Center, Boston, MA

Judith Jones, National Center for Children in Poverty, Columbia University, New York, NY

Lynn Kagan, Child Development and Social Policy, Yale University Bush Center, New Haven, CT

Sheila Kamerman, School of Social Work, Columbia University, New York, NY

Evelyn Kays-Battle, Reginald Lourie Center for Infants and Young Children, Rockville, MD

Steven Kelman, John F. Kennedy School of Government, Harvard University, Cambridge, MA

Richard Kinch, Johnson Foundation, Racine, WI

Thomas Langfitt, Pew Charitable Trust, Philadelphia, PA

Carol Larson, David and Lucile Packard Foundation, Los Altos, CA

Michael Levine, Carnegie Corporation of New York, New York, NY

Janet E. Levy, Joining Forces, Washington, DC

Joan Lipsitz, Lilly Endowment, Inc., Indianapolis, IN

Shelby Miller, Ford Foundation, New York, NY

Lyn Mortimer, Carnegie Corporation of New York, New York, NY

Richard P. Nathan, Rockefeller College, Albany, NY

Douglas Nelson, Annie E. Casey Foundation, CT

Billie K. Press, Reginald Lourie Center for Infants and Young Children, Rockville, MD

Beryl Radin, Washington Public Affairs Center, University of Southern California, Washington, DC

Harold Richman, Chapin Hall Center for Children, Chicago, IL

Gloria G. Rodriquez, AVANCE, San Antonio, TX

Ann Rosewater, Consultant, Atlanta, GA

Ellen Schall, National Center for Health Education, New York, NY

Ann Segal, Division of Children and Youth Policy, Department of Health and Human Services, Washington, DC

Ralph R. Smith, Philadelphia Children's Network, Philadelphia, PA

Rosalie Street, Friends of the Family, Baltimore, MD

Reed Tuckson, March of Dimes Birth Defects Foundation, White Plains, NY

Robert L. Wehling, Proctor & Gamble Company, Cincinnati, OH

Heather Weiss, Harvard Family Research Project, Cambridge, MA

Bernice Weissbourd, Family Focus, Evanston, IL

Donna Weston, Children Hospital Medical Center, Oakland, CA